THE BARCLAY GUIDE TO

Marketing
for the Small Business

LEN ROGERS

Published by

Copyright © Len Rogers 1990

First published 1990

Basil Blackwell Ltd
108 Cowley Road, Oxford, OX4 1JF, UK

Basil Blackwell, Inc.
3 Cambridge Center
Cambridge, Massachusetts 02142, USA

British Library Cataloguing in Publication Data

A CIP catalogue record for this book is available from
the British Library

Library of Congress Cataloging in Publication Data

Rogers, Len
The Barclays guide to marketing for the small business / Len Rogers.
p.   cm. – (Barclays small business series)
ISBN 0–631–17246–7   ISBN 0–631–17247–5 (pbk.)
1. Marketing–Management.   2. Small business–Management.
I. Title.   II. Series.
HF5415.13.R57 1990
658.8–dc20   89–18215 CIP

Typeset in 10½ on 12½pt Plantin
by Hope Services (Abingdon) Ltd
Printed in Great Britain by
T. J. Press Ltd, Padstow, Cornwall

Contents

Contents

Contents

Contents

Foreword

The last five years have seen a significant growth in the number of small businesses in all sectors of industry in the UK. Unfortunately they have also seen an increase in the numbers of problems encountered by those businesses. Often the problems could have been avoided with the right help and advice.

Barclays, in association with Basil Blackwell, is producing this series of guides to give that help and advice. They are comprehensive and written in a straightforward way. Each one has been written by a specialist in the field, in conjunction with Barclays Bank, and drawing on our joint expertise to ensure that the advice given is appropriate.

With the aid of these guides the businessman or woman will be better prepared to face the many challenges ahead, and, hopefully, will be better rewarded for their efforts.

George Cracknell
Director UK Business
Sector Services
Barclays Bank plc

Preface

Marketing for success

People who start their own businesses and make successes of them, do so not because they are good engineers, skilled craftsmen, or computer experts: they succeed because they are marketing people. They have found that they can supply something that will satisfy customers, and that the customers are prepared to pay them for it.

Your market

For the product or service you are offering, your market will consist of people: people as individuals or in groups; people as consumers, in private practice, in commerce, or in companies and organizations where they are employed to buy goods and services. Identifying the market for your product is crucial to your success.

Your product

The product or service is the most important factor in your business. If you have no product, you have nothing to sell; if you have nothing to sell, you can't make any money.

Price and profit

You make money from the price you charge for your product or service, and it will determine how much you sell and how much profit you make. To the extent that you price unwisely, you will affect profits and create dissatisfaction in your customers.

Expose yourself!

If your product just sits there doing nothing, it's a dead loss – to customers and to you. Expose it: get it in the right place at the right time. Your success lies in decent exposure of yourself and your product.

Shout it from the rooftops!

The man who whispers down a well about the goods he has to sell will never make as many dollars as he that climbs a tree and hollers.

Sell! Sell! Sell!

When all the marketers and planners have had their moment, and the production and finance problems have been dealt with, then someone, somewhere, has to go out and sell. It may be in the shop, in the home of a local resident, in the buyer's alcove of a small factory, or the office of a buying agent for a foreign customer. This selling activity takes place every day of the week and, because marketing is now a global business, it is done twenty-four hours a day, year in, year out.

Do it now!

It's not what you know, but what you *do* about what you know. *Do it now!*

Acknowledgements

I wish to thank the editors of *Business Week* and *The Economist* for some of the references made in the book, and Charles Batchelor of *Financial Times* for references to some of the experiences of small business people made in his regular column on marketing for small businesses.

LEN ROGERS

Luxembourg, 1990

Acknowledgements

I

The importance of marketing

Outline

This chapter reviews the contents of the guide and introduces some key ideas. We look at:

- the two meanings of the term 'marketing' and the importance of customers
- marketing mix, sales mix and product mix
- channels of distribution
- market segmentation
- market share
- market research
- competition

The small business

This guide to marketing is for the small business. Irrespective of the number of people employed in a company, most marketing practices are the same; only the scale differs.

Where appropriate, chapters start with applications relevant to the one-person or tiny company, and then discusses their adaptations for the larger company. If you are already working on your own or intend to do so, you will find that some of the material in the chapters deals with problems you will have to cope with later, as you grow.

What is marketing?

Marketing is concerned with supplying products and services to customers. It's more than just selling; it's finding out the real needs of potential customers and then satisfying those needs at a profit. It's supplying products and services that customers will buy, rather than trying to sell products that you happen to make. For this reason marketing really starts before the product is made.

Marketing has two main meanings: an organizational philosophy and a company function.

As an organizational philosophy, marketing is an all-embracing doctrine, and includes the 'customers' of all non-profit-making organizations such as churches, police forces, hospitals etc., as well as those of profit-seeking companies. It tends to be theoretical, and is the subject of much academic investigation.

As a company function, marketing includes a number of practical activities such as market research, product scheduling, advertising, promotion, selling and servicing, and has a similar degree of responsibility and authority to the production, finance and personnel functions.

The marketing mix

We are more concerned with the function of marketing and what we have to do to marketing-orient our business activities. The basis for these is the *marketing mix*, which can be reduced to a consideration of:

- product or service;
- price and profit structure;
- channels and methods used to distribute the products or supply the services to the ultimate user;
- selling procedures, and media used to promote the products;
- servicing of customers and products.

These are the five main internal activities – product, price, place, promotion and service – and they can be controlled by you. As well as being known as the marketing mix these are also referred to as the 4Ps+S.

Sound marketing mix making is the basis for successful marketing. By varying the combination of effort you apply to the five, you emphasize the importance you attach to each for any given market.

However, don't think of it as five ingredients of a cake mixture, and that by varying the quantities of flour, fat, sugar, eggs etc. you end up with a different cake. With the marketing mix ingredients it is not the quantities of each you use, or the resources you apply to them, but the combined degrees of importance you place on the five components.

The marketing mix approach combines practice with theory. You can quantify the importance of the promotion component by deciding the amount of money to be spent on it. To some extent you can quantify the price component by setting a high or low price to affect your profit, but you don't have to devote any resources to it.

You cannot so easily quantify the importance of product, place and service by applying resources to them. Some examples will clarify this.

A small company in Devon decides to market a range of women's beauty preparations made from locally grown herbs and natural products. The five marketing mix components will not have equal importance. The most important might be promotion, followed by product, distribution and price, with a little emphasis on service.

A biochemist who has developed over twenty different compounds for use in industry has a different marketing mix: product and service are regarded as crucial to success, distribution is important, and price and promotion are much less important.

Suppose the importance of the total marketing mix effort is regarded as 100 per cent. If the five components are considered to be equally important, each one is emphasized 20 per cent in the total marketing endeavours: the product would be equally important as its price, distribution, promotion and service.

This is not a definitive technique: there is no unique combination of the five components to suit a given market. You could market your product with a marketing mix that emphasizes price at, say, 75 per cent. A competitor could market a similar product but with a different mix, emphasizing promotion at 75 per cent. Both of you could achieve similar success in the market: you sell on price; your competitor sells with publicity.

As soon as you understand the marketing mix concept you can forget the percentage approach: it is used merely to explain it.

Consider the marketing mixes for a design service by a woman designer, a free-lance computer software programmer, a house-cleaning service, a one-man jobbing gardener and a tiny engineering company.

Common to all is high emphasis on product and service in their marketing efforts, but they would have different views about the importance of price, promotion and distribution for their respective products.

Product

Your products and services define your opportunities for sales and profits. Without a product or service you have nothing to market. But you should not develop products in isolation; they must be put together with a specific market in mind, and in line with your overall objectives. Customers should want to buy your products or use your services because you give better value.

Your total range of products is your *product mix*, and should be related to your *sales mix* – the different quantities of products purchased by your customers. However, while you decide the product mix, your customers decide your sales mix.

Using marketing to power your business will ensure that your product mix is relevant to your sales mix: you are not trying to increase sales of the least profitable products; you are not prolonging the life of a product at the expense of more profitable opportunities; you don't introduce a new product without adequate knowledge of the market.

Price

You will stay in business as long as your customers are prepared to pay your price. Price provides you with profit, and profit not only pays today's expenses, it provides a reserve for tomorrow when business may not be so buoyant. Profit indicates your success in finding, satisfying and keeping customers.

Pricing is a flexible marketing tool. So flexible in fact that it is often used indiscriminately: sales increase; profits fall. If you are going to compete on price, you must be efficient and ready for the inevitable counter-attacks from competitors.

Price may be set towards the ceiling or the floor – a high price or a low price policy. Chapter 4 will help you decide where between the ceiling and the floor you should set your price.

Place

Having your products in the factory, lock-up workshop or garage after they are made is of no use to a potential customer in another town. Unless you are re-creating old masters, customers are most unlikely to come searching for your work. Products will only sell if they are in the right place for customers to buy.

Good distribution is having the goods in the *right place* at the *right time*. Applying good marketing practice, you should also have the *right products* there at the *right price*.

You can distribute your products in three main ways:

- direct to the user;
- through middlemen such as stockists or retailers;
- through more than one middleman, such as factors, concessionnaires, wholesalers, retailers and franchisees.

The small business is likely to concentrate on a local area and deal directly with the user. Although the closer you get to the user, the more costly it is, you have greater control over the selling process. Distribution is the subject of chapter 5.

Promotion: advertising

You may be ready to sell the fruits of your labours, but if customers are not ready to buy, there's little point in advertising. You must advertise at the right time – and the right time for customers, not necessarily for you.

You must advertise in the right places, that is, using the right media. No matter how good your product and how brilliant your publicity, if you advertise to the wrong people, you won't sell much.

It's easy to spend money on advertising, so it is essential to get the most out of what you do spend. The five main media are:

- all forms of press – newspapers, magazines, technical and professional journals;
- commercial television;
- outdoor publicity;
- radio;
- cinema.

Each of these is monitored by independent research organizations which record the amount of money spent by companies on their products in the main media and a selection of subsidiary ones. So you can get hold of the information. There are scores of other advertising possibilities more attractive to the small business. They include exhibitions, direct mail, contests, sponsorship, competitions, point-of-sale displays, merchandising, and sales literature.

Whether you use word-of-mouth, small advertisements, radio announcements or commercial television, you must tell your prospective customers how they can obtain the benefits of your product or service. There are five main points to consider:

- To whom are you appealing?
- What are you aiming to achieve?
- Why should the prospective customers buy from you?
- What proofs of the product benefits can be offered?
- How is the product or service to be identified with *you*?

We shall be looking at advertising in more detail in chapter 6 and promotion in chapter 7.

Promotion: personal selling

In the context of marketing mix, promotion includes personal selling as well as advertising and publicity. If you sell your products by mail order, you won't need sales people; every other method requires someone to go out and sell.

In the early days of the small business, it's usually the owner who has to do the selling. If the owner is also making the goods or supplying the service, it's a bit like taking penalties and running like mad into the goal-mouth to save them!

There is one large compensating fact: selling is dealing with customers, and customers provide profits for the business. Everything done inside the company costs money (more so in a large company). All the production people, engineers, technicians, scientists, the accountants, sales people, administrators etc. cost a great deal of money. None of them makes any profit. It is only when you go outside the company and find customers that you make profits.

The small business cannot afford to employ sales people until it is established and has sufficient profits flowing from sales to carry them while they are developing their own sales. This still leaves us with the present selling task to be done.

Sales provide turnover; turnover provides profit. Therefore the costs of selling must, sooner or later, be related to profit.

The appointment of sales agents, though less satisfactory, will cause less financial problems. Chapter 8 should help you to sell more effectively and know what to look for when employing sales people.

Service

The fate of a small business often rests solely on its ability to give good service. What customers regard as 'good value' is often, in reality, the accompanying service.

A small firm of furniture removers on the South Coast, which started with one van, has grown in size and standing because of its service to customers. Their repeat business is practically nil, but their reputation for satisfying the customer is widely known. This has been achieved by attention to detail, from the colour and cleanliness of the inside and outside of their vans, the care and attention to customers' property, to the style of their letter headings and presentation of documents.

Their prices are much the same as their competitors, but their competitors just move furniture; this small company has built up its reputation by giving service.

Most sales require some service before the actual order is placed. If you have to prepare quotations or tenders to get orders, this is pre-sales service, which is not paid for but has to be carried in general overhead expenses. Unless you control this it can get out of hand and erode your profits.

When your agents and sales people are progressing sales with potential customers, they need an adequate sales kit to do the job. A sales person who cannot deal with the majority of customers' enquiries without recourse to you when they are raised is not being serviced adequately.

After-sales service helps to keep the product sold. The type of product will dictate the kind and amount of service necessary to keep buyers happy.

For the small business, service is not only the most important element in determining success, it is also the one thing at which it can excel.

The subject of service will be dealt with in much greater detail in chapter 9.

Opportunities and targets

The environment in which you are operating contains the external factors over which you have little or no control. Nevertheless, they offer you opportunities for success. You must learn to cope with them.

What customers regard as value, and what they buy, is decisive – it determines the nature of your business, what you produce, and whether or not you will prosper. Customers are the foundation of your business: without them you will fail. This is the real purpose of marketing: to find customers. Profit reflects your success in finding and satisfying them.

Your products must be related to your target markets, and attractive enough in performance and price for customers to buy. A market consists of people with needs, the means to satisfy those needs, and the willingness to satisfy them. Such needs may or may not be known by them; two of your main marketing tasks are to ascertain those needs and then focus your products and services on the target market. This provides marketing with its opportunities: developing products and services to satisfy the perceived needs of customers, and supplying them at prices that will yield profit to your business.

If you give insufficient thought to customers' needs, but offer products that you have developed in your spare room, garage, workshop or factory, rather than having designed them for a target market, you will be outsold by competitors who are marketing-oriented.

Market segmentation

A market segment is a part of the total market. For a small business, it is seldom possible to tackle the whole market; it has to be divided into smaller, more manageable parts. These must be substantial enough to provide adequate business for all competitors.

Obviously, the best segment for a small business just starting out is a geographic one, as near as possible to base: it can be clearly defined and the customers readily and quickly approached. The more that customers are dispersed throughout the market, the less it favours the small company.

Consider the marketing problems confronting a small business that has been set up in the Scottish Highlands to market hand-made horn and bone buttons. Segmenting the market geographically would be of little use because the nearest customer is over 150 km away, the furthest nearly 1,000 km. In fact the market for this specialized craft is dispersed throughout the UK. Considerable effort and time is necessary to find potential customers and service them.

If you have a product for a dispersed segment, you should capitalize on the knowledge you acquire about the segment. Any future product development should be carried out with that segment in mind. In this way you can build a large share of a small market. Segmentation is vital to the success of a small company: the subject is discussed in detail in chapter 5.

Sales forecasting

Until you make a sales forecast, you cannot do any real planning. If you have no idea of the number of products or the amount of service you hope to sell over the next year, you won't know how much money you'll need to finance the operation. You won't know what materials to order, or how many products to make. You won't know what accessories you'll need, or whether you even have the time to achieve the forecast.

The sales forecast is the primary planning tool of your business. All planning starts with an implicit or explicit forecast of sales. Even a vague forecast is better than none at all; at least you will have something to start with. Make your forecast for a period of up to a year, and break it down into months or weeks. Allow for any likely variation of sales due to seasonal fluctuations. Your forecast should be in terms of value or volume – whichever is more appropriate to your business. As soon as you start operations, record your progress against forecast and make any adjustments in your marketing efforts.

A sales forecast is really an estimate of the share of the total market you hope to achieve. If you think forecasting sales is difficult, wait till you try to forecast the total market and a market share!

Market share

Getting a reasonable share of the available market is the aim of any business. While this applies equally to the small business, determining market share is a far from easy task. The main difficulty lies in defining the market accurately.

What is the market for a one-woman company offering a book-keeping and financial service to retailers? Is she giving a daily, weekly or monthly service? Will it include preparation of VAT returns? Will she prepare final accounts and deal with the tax inspector? And will it be all retailers, or a selection? Should they be split into different-sized shops? They could be subdivided into type of products sold. Maybe they should be categorized by type, and her market is independent stores. But there are thousands of those. Perhaps her real market is independent stores within a specific area near to her base.

The more detailed the definition of the product in terms of what the customer is buying, and the more accurate a description of the customer, the more you are defining the true market for that product.

The woman supplying the retail financial service has an actual market considerably smaller than the total market. She may have a very small share of the total market, but a large share of the market in which she is operating.

Another difficulty lies in the terms used to define market share. Three small businesses supplying a similar product share a total market of £63,000 as in exhibit 1.1.

Company	Turnover	Market share
A	£15,000	24%
B	£29,250	46%
C	£18,750	30%
	£63,000	100%

Exhibit 1.1 Market shares

On taking a close look into these three companies we find that their products, though apparently similar, differ in some aspects. Company A is selling mainly on price, and has sold to more outlets than the other two put together. The additional figures in exhibit 1.2 illustrate the difficulties of defining market share.

Company	Price	No. of outlets	Market share	Sales of products	Market share	Turnover	Market share
A	£50	52	51%	300	30%	£15,000	24%
B	£65	29	28%	450	45%	£29,250	46%
C	£75	21	21%	250	25%	£18,750	30%

Exhibit 1.2 Different market shares

While company B has the highest market share in value and volume sales of products, company A has a higher market share of outlets. It is not unusual to find two competitors both claiming to be the market leader: one has the highest volume sales; the other has the highest turnover.

Don't spend too much of your time embroiled with statistics and forecasts, but aim to organize your business within sound marketing principles. Be aware of what you should be doing, but don't be worried if in the early days you find that this is not always possible.

For example, whenever you make a sales forecast you should make a market forecast so that you have a *market share* forecast. As you become more experienced in marketing your product or service your forecasting will improve.

This is important, as you can see from the following illustration. A small company in Bridgwater, Somerset, makes tables and chairs of special local materials such that they have a relatively small total market for their products. Exhibit 1.3 shows their forecast market share for a year. Their actual sales for the year are given in exhibit 1.4. This shows that they sold above their forecast for chairs, but below for tables.

	Tables	Chairs
Sales forecast for 1987	150	900
Market segment forecast sales	10,000	30,000
Forecast market share	1.5%	3%

Exhibit 1.3 Estimated market share

	Tables	Chairs
Sales forecast for 1987	150	900
Company sales for 1987	125	1,040
Percentage of forecast	83%	115%

Exhibit 1.4 Percentage forecast achieved

The value of having market segment estimates with company sales forecasts can be seen in exhibit 1.5. What was thought to have been a good selling job for chairs was not; share of the market segment was estimated at 3 per cent, but only 2 per cent was achieved. On the other hand an apparently poor result for tables was actually a good effort: market share was 2.5 per cent compared with the forecast 1.5 per cent.

Marketing research

You must obtain information on the market, but the mere possession of accurate data does not, in itself, ensure success.

	Tables	Chairs
Market segment sales for 1987	5,000	50,000
Company sales for 1987	125	1,040
Estimated market share	1.5%	3%
Market share for year	2.5%	2%
Variation in market share	+1%	−1%

Exhibit 1.5 Actual market shares

Marketing research is to business what military intelligence is to a general, or a dictionary to a writer. No general would start a battle without obtaining knowledge that was as complete as possible about the opposing forces. And all the stories that have ever been written are to be found in a dictionary; it is the selection and order of the words that have been arranged by the authors!

Marketing research is concerned with investigations into three main areas: the product, distribution and the market. For the findings of any research to represent the facts accurately it should be done on a formal basis by people independent of your business. This avoids bias creeping into the results by respondents telling you what they think you want to hear, such as, 'Your product is the best I've tried,' 'Yes, I'd buy some if they were available,' and 'Let me know when you start your service, I'll have it.'

While information on the market, competitive products and distribution is vital to any business, the cost of getting independent market intelligence is prohibitive for the small company. Yet even the company without sufficient sales turnover to require registration for VAT needs market data.

Suppose you were about to start a business cleaning windows, operating a hairdressing salon, growing tomatoes, making decorative brooches, writing computer software, supplying secretarial services, running a vegetarian restaurant, or some equally small operation: to do so without having a clear idea of your potential market would be folly. But to spend the kind of money necessary to obtain unbiased answers and opinions would probably mean that you would have none left to conduct the business.

This has actually happened in the author's experience. A small businessman in Reigate, Surrey, spent his first few months finding out all he could about customers and competitors. He obtained almost complete knowledge of the market. Anything he was not sure of he re-checked. He knew his competitors' product ranges, turnover and profits; he knew their prices and discounts, the amounts spent on advertising, the main customers and how sales were conducted. He used a large amount of his available money in establishing the facts. Having obtained all the knowledge, he couldn't afford to start his business. After many months of market research he was like a new dictionary lying discarded on a shelf.

The cost of obtaining a market survey must obviously be related to the size of the 'small' business.

Competitive and competing products

Your product will undoubtedly have competition.

Competitive products are those which are similar or identical to yours and are directly comparable: they are relatively easy to recognize and describe. Thus the different window cleaners in an area are offering a competitive service; the local craft shops found in tourist areas are selling competitive products. Different makes of lampshades are competitive with each other.

Competing products are often difficult to identify because they do not always appear to be in competition with your product. They are different products or services which tend to give customers equal satisfaction, and they compete for customers' available money.

Lampshades made from locally-woven fabric, and decorative stones gathered from the nearby beach, shaped and polished are competing products; locally made ice cream and nationally advertised confectionery are competing; a boat trip to the island to view the seals, and a round of miniature golf are competing services. Customers can neither buy nor do everything they want because their money and time are limited. They have to make choices from products and services that are competing with each other.

You should summarize the main competitive products currently on the market; if the information is available and you have thoroughly investigated the situation you should also list any likely future competitive offers. This is particularly important if a high, or new, technology is involved: you should be able to describe the market in considerable detail.

You start to 'think marketing' when you list the products likely to compete with yours. It's not easy, but the exercise will give you a clearer insight into the market.

How to be successful

People who start their own business have a great advantage over those employed in other companies. They are not inhibited by an authoritative establishment; there are no preconceived ideas, no staff that have grown up with the company, no production methods that have been in use for years, no rigid structure. They can make a success of their business because they can start marketing from the word go.

It is not because a man is a good engineer, a highly qualified scientist, or a talented craftsman that he becomes the owner of a successful business; it is not because a woman is a creative designer, an experienced negotiator, or skilled computer programmer that she is able to run her own show.

The people who prosper in business are dedicated marketing people. They have found or created something – a product or service – that they can supply to customers who are willing to pay them, and so enable profits to be made.

The key to the continued development and success of your business will be sound, profitable marketing. Marketing does not exist in a vacuum between sales and production: it is the total activity of an organization, whether that organization is a large public multinational, a medium-sized limited company, a private family business, or *one person alone*.

Key points

- Focus all your business decisions on the customer.
- Successful marketing means relating the product, price, place, promotion and service to the customer.
- Product, service and flexibility provide the small business with its main advantages.
- Start operations near to your base.
- Get everyone in your company involved in marketing.

2

The market

Outline

A market consists basically of people, but they are people in different circumstances and groups. The basic driving force that creates markets is needs. We look at:

- actual, possible, potential and latent markets
- analysing customers' needs
- defining a company's market
- planning for product/markets
- essential market research for the small business
- sources of market information
- the industrial buying decision-making unit

What is a market?

A market for a product or service consists of people with *needs*, the *means* to satisfy those needs, and the *willingness* to satisfy them.

Everyone has needs; you, your family, your friends, your colleagues and professional buyers. However, to satisfy these needs, not only is it necessary to have the funds or credit facilities, but there must also be a willingness to buy.

Undoubtedly there are people who have a need for your product and are willing to buy it, but if they don't have the money, you make no sales. This is a *possible market*.

There are also people who have the funds and a need for your product, but are unwilling to buy it; you will make no sales until their attitude is changed. This is a *potential market*.

And then there are people who have the money and are willing to spend it, but if they have no need of your product, no sales will result. This may be described as a *latent market*.

While possible, potential and latent markets offer varying degrees of attraction, your primary interest must be in a current market with active demand. Demand for your product or service will only be effective if all three criteria are present: a need, the money to satisfy that need and the willingness to satisfy it.

How to find your market

Of the three criteria, the most important is need. A market will not exist unless potential customers have a need, irrespective of whether they are aware of it or not.

People with size 10 feet have no need of size 7 shoes; bald-headed men don't need haircuts; those with first-class eyesight have no need of reading spectacles; non-smokers have no need of cigarettes; people in houses with oil-fired central heating and no open fireplaces have no need of coal; offices with their own staff canteens are unlikely to need a lunchtime sandwich service.

Some needs are essential to life: air, water, food etc. Some are essential to industry: raw materials and fuel. They are essential in the sense that, without them, life and industry as we know it could not exist.

Other products are not so vital but are highly desirable: shelter, clothing, transport, communications, metal tools and energy. In a modern industrialized society the high standard of living requires electric lights, vacuum cleaners, refrigerators, washing machines, telephones, telefax, photocopiers, internal combustion engines, pumps and computers to control air line bookings, bank accounts, income tax, dental and hospital records. Obviously these are needs of an advanced order.

To make a market for your product or service it must satisfy a need. You can worry later about whether people know they have a need of it, whether they have the money, or whether they are willing to buy. First there must be the need.

Varying degrees of need

People have different needs because of their circumstances and personal preferences. Where people need the same type of product the intensity of the need will vary with the people concerned. A particular product may be extremely important to some people – they must have it; the same product will be less critical to others, who will buy it when convenient. Similarly, offices and factories have different degrees of need for the same products and services. There is thus a hierarchy of needs for both consumers and industry.

Ordinary people – consumers – each have a list, usually in their minds, of things they propose to acquire. At the top of the list are their vital needs; others, less important, come a little further down; some things that they can only hope to obtain later in life appear towards the bottom of the list. It is the same with industrial organizations, although they are perhaps a little more formally organized. The board of management will have a number of items in their pending file earmarked for future acquisition.

Markets therefore consist of people with varying needs. These may be graded as 'essential needs', 'wants' and 'desires'. Exhibit 2.1 shows some products and services with their general degree of need.

	Consumer	Industrial
Need	Air Water Food	Raw materials Fuel Fire extinguishers
Want	Shelter Clothes Hair-dressing Satellite TV?	Tools Transport Air-conditioning?
Desire	Motor car? Country cottage?	Computer-aided design? Robotized manufacturing?

Exhibit 2.1 Hierarchy of needs

The products classified as consumer and industrial needs are fairly obvious, although air is only a salable product to divers, astronauts and those who need a portable supply of it. As you descend through the hierarchy of needs, however, you enter areas of conjecture. Where, for example, would you place consumer television sets? And would you differentiate between monochrome and colour sets? Is satellite television a want or a desire product? It could well be regarded by one segment of the market as a want, and by another segment (probably much larger) as a desire product. Air-conditioning might be considered an industrial want, but for many modern industries – especially some of the high technology manu-facturing plants – it is a necessity.

The classification of needs, wants and desires must be reappraised for different markets. The market in the south-east of England is different from the market in Scotland; the conurbation of Liverpool is dissimilar from the conurbation of Plymouth. Even in the so-called Common Market there are disparate markets: the market in south-west England is quite distinct from the market in south-west France.

Think about your own product or service and make an initial appraisal of its degree of need by the market you have in mind.

Less need, more effort

The effort necessary to sell a product is indicated by how much the product is needed by the market. The closer that customers come to consider it to be a desire product, the greater will be the selling effort required. You have to persuade people of the benefits of acquiring a desire product, irrespective of whether it is a consumer or an industrial product.

Need products have little, if any, sales resistance to be overcome, but because such products are in great demand many suppliers are prepared to satisfy customers' needs. For high-need products and services the emphasis is not on selling, but on marketing.

Defining your market

Defining your market means deciding what kinds of people or organizations could possibly buy your product, and narrowing it down to a manageable yet sizeable number of prospects. If you have a product, such as soap, that could be used by all consumers the total market is the population of the country. If the product is of interest mainly to adult males – say, handmade brier pipes – then the total market is the number of men in the population over the age of 16. But if you considered either of these total markets as your market, to be successful you would need a deep faith and a deep pocket.

First you quantify your market by reducing the total market to what is feasible with your resources. Then you qualify it by relating the product to the potential customers and judging their degree of need for it.

Suppose that you intend to market a high-quality consumer article. The UK market consists of over 55 million people, who live in 21 million households. About 45 million are adults over 15 years of age. Your product could be used by all adults over 15, so you have a lovely big market of 45 million potential buyers. Then you remember that your product will be used in the home, not personally by individuals, so you revise your market downwards. It's still huge – 21 million.

There's no way that you could tackle such a huge market: your production is limited, and you have no staff to help you or sales people to get orders. The number must be further refined. Your first efforts could be made locally, so you decide that the city where you live is your initial market. It has a population of about 135,000, so, by a simple calculation, if 55 million live in 21 million households (i.e. is 2.6 people per household) the approximate number of households in your city is about 52,000.

Market planning should be for *product/markets*, and not for the market or product in isolation. You now qualify your market by deciding that the product is a consumer 'want', and will appeal mainly to managers in senior positions, professional people and those categorized as upper middle class. From sources that will be described later in this guide you find that about 2.5 per cent of the population is in this category. You estimate that your initial market is 2.5 per cent of 52,000 – about 1,300 in your city. In these calculations, numbers and percentages of population and households have been mixed, but the variations are not critical.

Willingness cannot be ascertained

We have already discussed customers' needs; by now you should have analysed your product from the viewpoint of the customer, and clarified what you are selling and what the customer is buying.

When investigating your potential market to determine likely demand, you will be able to find out two things: whether your proposed customers have a need for your product, and whether they have the means to buy it. What you cannot determine is the number who will actually buy. Many have a need and can afford it, but when it comes to putting the money down the situation changes. You'll get enthusiastic responses such as: 'Yes! I'll certainly buy one!' and, 'Splendid, I'm sure that we'll benefit from your product.' You'll also get: 'Let me know as soon as you are able to supply.'

People have scales of preferences. If your product is somewhere near the top of their list – that is, a real need product – they will be willing to buy. If it is not near the top of the list, the purchase is likely to be postponed. What they said 'Yes' to yesterday becomes 'Perhaps' today; 'Let's leave it for the time being' tomorrow; and 'No' in a month's time.

Willingness to buy can only be tested in the cold reality of the actual market when products are competing with one another, fighting to gain the attention and eventual votes of customers.

Don't build your marketing plans on promises and faith, but on facts. The situation you find in the market will indicate your general marketing strategy. You may need to direct your efforts to educating the customer in the product's use and the arousal of needs, or to overcoming unwillingness and persuading them to buy from you.

Marketing research

Before your plans are too far advanced, and certainly before you enter into any commitments, you must obtain objective data on the market you propose to enter. The following eight factors of marketing will guide you in your research:

- the product – what is the customer actually buying?
- the size and average value of a typical sale;
- the area of proposed operations;
- the competition in the proposed area;
- the present methods of distribution;

- the strength of the selling effort required;
- the cost of the selling effort;
- the after-sales service required.

By gathering all possible information on each of these, you will build sufficient marketing intelligence on which to base your operations.

Essential research for the small company

Market research is time-consuming but necessary. There are plenty of data, surveys and reports published by trade journals, banks, the Department of Trade and Industry, and various trade associations: much of it is free. You can also obtain a lot of sound information simply by phoning sources.

You should already have carried out some product research, otherwise you wouldn't be starting your own business. We assume that your product is satisfactory, will do what you think it will do and, if appropriate, has been thoroughly tested. You should also have compared it with competitive products for quality and performance.

Some of the above factors are the subjects of separate chapters in this guide. Such is the nature of marketing that it is not possible to keep everything in watertight compartments: subjects and topics continually overlap. If a factor has been expanded in its own chapter, only the main market research points are noted here, but, where necessary, important details are illustrated with an example or are examined more fully.

Make a list of the market information you consider to be *essential* to your business under the headings of the eight factors, selecting those that are relevant.

The product

Classify your product in marketing terms; who is likely to buy it and who will use it? Are buyer and user the same person? Avoid classifying products in purely academic terms, or categorizing them without having reasons why. Regard your product in terms of what the customer is buying, and whether or not it is a need, a want or a desire. How are customers' needs, wants and desires currently being satisfied? What advantages will they gain by acquiring your product?

Do you have a complete range of styles or models? Will the product be able to develop its own strong image or brand name? What is the performance of your product compared with competitive offers? What will it do that other products won't? Does it have any unique selling points?

Size and average value of sale

An ordinary packet of washing detergent is about the size of a large book; and you will have an idea of its value. Consider the powder when purchased by the retailer: because it is bought in dozens, each sale is likely to be equal in size to several bookcases, while its value will be many times the price paid by the housewife. Now think about the powder when purchased by the wholesaler: the sale is as large as a small library (certainly the size of the truck in which it is delivered), and its value is many times that paid by the retailer. It's the same detergent, but at each level of transaction the size and value is different.

What will be the size and likely value of sale for your product? Your answers will indicate how you have to distribute and sell it.

Suppose you were setting up a small furniture business, or a resin-bonded glass-fibre boat-building yard. The size and value of the average sale will both be large, and will influence how you market your products. You couldn't sell them around the local housing estate; you would have to market them through trade channels.

You might be starting a business manufacturing specialist audio cassettes; or domestic brushes; or fabric bags, aprons and covers; or you might be raising herb plants etc. The size and value of these products would be small, and the marketing methods for them different from those for large, costly products.

If you are starting a service operation, such as a print business; a wedding ceremony recordist; a dry-cleaner; a beauty salon; a photocopying bureau; a specialist shop etc., the average value of sale would be more important because physical size has no relevance.

The significance of considering the size and value of average sale is that you see the transaction from the viewpoint of the customer; it is the size and value of the *purchase*.

Area of operations

The extent and make-up of the geographical area of your proposed business will reveal a lot of relevant data.

How wide will you have to spread your net to make your operation a viable business? There must be sufficient potential trade in the area to provide you *and* all your competitors with a reasonable, profitable turnover. If you have to visit potential customers in the area, the farther you operate from your base the more costly it will be.

With some products and services, such as shops, art galleries, cafés, hairdressing salons, restaurants and hotels, customers come to you. The total market is related to the area from which you can reasonably expect to attract customers. This is the *catchment area* of the business.

A specialist shop, such as one offering a framing service for photographs, prints and paintings, will require a larger catchment area than a shop offering groceries. The degree of need for the product or service and how often it is purchased will determine the number of shops that exist. There are more grocery stores than framing service shops, more chemists than print shops, more cafés than restaurants, and so on.

If you have to rely on a catchment area, you will need to assess it in detail. Take an extreme example. Suppose you were thinking of opening a grocery store specializing in Asian foodstuffs: your catchment area must contain sufficient potential customers. You couldn't expect to open such a shop, say, in the middle of Dartmoor, because the number of customers to make it a feasible proposition live too far away. You could work twelve hours or more a day, stay open from early morning until late at night: you wouldn't make enough money to live because your catchment area does not have adequate potential business.

Other propositions are not so transparent, and yet the area of operations, or catchment area, is sometimes crucial to the viability of a business.

Let us assume that you are proposing to open a restaurant: from how far away is it likely to attract custom? Its catchment area will comprise all people living within a certain radius who eat out from time to time. But how large a radius? How many people? In a densely populated area the radius will be smaller than in one that is sparsely populated. The important factor is the number of potential eaters-out, and the problem is best approached from the opposite direction: how many customers are needed in the catchment area to make the restaurant a viable proposition?

We appraise the product. What is the customer buying; a quick, low-priced snack or a leisurely, gastronomic meal? And, how many can be served during a meal-time? Say your restaurant will have a medium-priced menu of English and French dishes, and can serve fifty people for lunch or dinner. You need to know how many times a year people in the area eat out and, from the sources given in this guide, you decide that they visit a restaurant, on average, six times a year. You assume that your customers will be couples rather than individuals. How far will they travel to a restaurant?

A general tendency should be noted here. People who visit restaurants expect to have a reasonable meal, sometimes an expensive meal, but they do not travel very far just to eat hamburgers. The further they have to go for a meal, the more the standard of the meal must justify the journey. Thus the product will influence the area of your market and potential clientele. You decide that the restaurant will attract people living within a radius of ten miles. The population in this area is 80,000; what percentage of them eat out?

Some guesses are made. If 5 per cent eat out from time to time, this is a total potential of 4,000 who visit a restaurant, on average, six times a year, which is equivalent to 24,000 meals. In the area there are several other cafés and restaurants but only three that could be considered to be competitive with your restaurant. This indicates that the 4,000 potential customers might patronize the four restaurants, and provide an average of 6,000 meals for each restaurant.

Your restaurant will seat fifty people, and is open for lunch and dinner, 300 days a year. The total possible number of meals you could serve is $300 \times 2 \times 50 = 30,000$ meals. Using the 6,000 average, the patronage of your restaurant is estimated to be 6,000/30,000, which is 20 per cent; 80 per cent of the time you are not making any money.

The 6,000 possible meals represent an average of five per meal-time, ten a day, or sixty a week. These meals are likely to be concentrated at the weekend, so it would only need a full restaurant on Saturday night to leave just ten people to eat with you during the rest of the week! Staff will become rather bored.

These are the bare statistics based on what is reasonably possible at an average rate. If the number of people who eat out has been overestimated, or you are unable to compete with other restaurants, revenue will be lower and your prospects bleaker. The point is that a benchmark has been established, and it would appear that the catchment area is not large enough to support another restaurant.

When considering the area of your operations, market-orient your approach by asking: how large an area is necessary to support the proposed business? First ascertain the 'population' in the area, and gradually refine this number to arrive at a figure relevant to your business. The population will be the total number of people, factories, offices, shops, garages, hotels, or whatever is the unit in which you are interested.

Finding out about your market

If your appraisal of the figures indicates that the potential market may be too small, you must find out more about it. Increase your market research: conduct a field survey.

For the proposed restaurant, this would entail visiting each of the others and making qualitative assessments, observing everything from the time you arrive.

How were you received? Were you shown to your table or directed to the bar? Are the chairs firm and well upholstered, or worn, too soft or uncomfortable? What is the quality of the cutlery, crockery, glasses and table linen? Are paper or linen napkins used? How many people were there? How strong are the relationships between the staff and clientele? What is the standard of cuisine? Is the quality and portions of food above average? Was your meal cooked individually for you, or were you served from food that had been kept hot? Was the service professional and in line with the type of meal? Was the bill what you expected, or were there additions for so-called extras?

The answers to these and other questions will give you a first-hand evaluation of your competitors. If you judge the competition to be poor, then a small catchment area might not be a deterrent to an enthusiastic and competent newcomer.

As you investigate your proposed market to determine numbers of potential customers and how well their needs are currently being satisfied, you will discover other valuable data. If there are a lot of competitors, prices will probably be keen. This will mean low unit profits, and unless you can achieve high volume sales total profits will be low.

If there are not many competitors selling a product similar to yours, this could be an ill omen. Your natural enthusiasm for your product may have blinded you to the fact that others are not so eager for it or, worse still, do not really need it.

Products are made obsolete by the introduction of new methods. It is difficult to purchase replacements and spare parts for many products beyond a certain age. Gas mantles for gas lighting will now only be found in shops catering for caravan accessories. And if you have an old fountain pen, to buy a replacement rubber ink sac these days means ordering from specialist suppliers. And it is now reported to be impossible to buy ribbons for mechanical typewriters in many parts of America because they have been overtaken by electronic machines and word processors.

If you find only a few competitors in the market for a product, this must ring a warning bell: investigate the situation in depth if you are contemplating entering that market.

Competition in the area

In contrast, when surveying your proposed area of operations, you may unearth a number of competitors. Not every competitor is necessarily strong in every area, and you should determine not only how many competitors there are, but their relative strengths.

If you have to rely on a catchment area, your business is obviously restricted to an area near to your base. But for all types of business it is sensible to develop sales near to the source of production or service. It takes less time to win customers and is less costly to supply and service them.

Once you have the area in mind, assess all the competitive activities: products, price structures, advertising, promotional activities, and how the products are distributed and transported. Obtain copies of all sales literature and, if appropriate, ascertain what servicing arrangements exist.

Present methods of distribution

When reviewing the area of operations you will discover the various distribution methods used by your competitors. You can assume that the methods they use have been tried and tested, and are effective. You would be a very adventurous person to ignore what has obviously been successful. But this shouldn't prevent you from trying new ways or even breaking new ground. Don't be blinkered into following the same pattern simply because 'It has always been done that way'. It is new thinking that wins new business.

There is a great deal more to be said on the subject of distribution, and we shall look at it in detail in chapter 5.

Strength of the selling effort required

As you gather data from your proposed market you will begin to appreciate how strong your *selling effort* will have to be to gain a foothold. In later chapters we shall explore at length the fire-power of personal selling and publicity. The market exploration stage is a fact-finding operation.

The easiest information to obtain is the amount of advertising by competitors. Get hold of all the local papers; look at the outdoor poster sites; retain every bit of publicity that arrives through your letter-box. Engage the help of relatives and friends to collect as much literature and advertising on competitive products or services as possible. Read the small classified ads in local papers, the national advertisers in the daily papers, and take note of the increasing use of facsimile machines and electronic mail.

Once you have an estimate of the total number of potential customers you will have a firm idea of the strength of selling effort necessary. To sell to 5,000 people or companies will cost much more than selling to 500. Yet you may need to sell to 5,000 to stand a chance of succeeding in your venture. The strength of the selling effort needed will have a direct effect on your costs.

One small businessman in High Wycombe, Bucks, started an anti-theft service to motorists, offering to etch the glass of their cars with the registration number. After one or two abortive efforts with small adverts in the local paper he realized that a much stronger selling effort was required.

The area is densely populated so he decided to call on potential customers every evening, and, if an order was obtained, arrange to mark their car windows at the weekend. The strength of the selling effort was high, but it generated a lot of business. Later he expanded by offering the service in supermarket car-parks while customers did their shopping.

He successfully competes with another organization in the area because he has judged the correct selling effort needed.

There is a sequel to this event which might be of interest to small business people who do not see the UK coastline as a barrier to expansion. A visitor from the USA saw this number etched on the windscreen and said that such a service did not exist in the States. He found sources for the small compressors and materials needed, returned to his home in California, and promptly started operations there. An added sophistication is that every car marked has its registration number recorded on computer. Anyone buying a car with its windows marked is able to obtain the history of the car from the computer bureau.

A different strength of sales effort was required in the States, and many weeks were spent selling the idea to police forces, highway patrols, insurance companies, consumer associations, women's groups and large garage groups.

Cost of the selling effort

Once you have judged what strength of sales effort is needed, how much time is required for personal selling, what distances have to be travelled, what expenses are likely to be involved, what weight of advertising is advisable, all these can be costed. At this stage you may need to have trade-offs. You are unlikely to be able to undertake everything you think necessary, so you must cut your garment according to the available cloth. We shall look at costs later in the guide.

After-sales service required

If you are supplying a service, you should already be attuned to the need to provide a comprehensive before-, during- and after-sales service to customers. If, however, you are about to start producing a product that will require after-sales service, you will find that getting the product into the hands of the user is one task, but providing adequate service is another operation.

Supplying a service should be a profitable exercise, but you will need sufficient products in use and out of the guarantee period before you can develop a beneficial service activity.

In your assessment of the market you can forecast the number of likely sales and calculate on a month-to-month basis the numbers of products that will become servicing targets after the guarantee period. The more you sell, the more you may need to service.

Regard this after-sales service as a future commitment to your customers. You will be able to estimate the size of the task during your initial appraisal of the market. When sales actually start, keep a running total of that commitment and its likely cost. As we shall see in chapter 4, which deals with pricing, your price structure must take this into consideration.

Sources of information

Obtain as much data as you can with the phone and by letter. Trade and technical publications can be especially helpful to the small business. Only use an independent consultant if there are vital questions left to be answered after your own investigations. Exhibit 2.2 shows a typical list edited from an actual research project carried out for a small company by the author. Question 3, 6, 7 and 8 required investigations in the field.

The finest free source for data on your market is your local reference library. Reference librarians are mines of information: if the facts exist they know where to find them, and they have a national network of sources. There is no need in this guide to list the mass of data that are available from government departments, local government offices, trade associations etc. It would take a great many pages and most of it will not be applicable to your business. Focus on the data you need, and ask the reference librarian.

Questions to be answered in the research

(1) What is the estimated size in volume and value (broken down by region and type of end-user) for 1988?
(2) What has been the trend of sales for all competitive products over the past five years?
(3) How is the trend identified in question 2 likely to develop to 1991?
(4) Who are the suppliers of 80 per cent of the market, and where are they located?
(5) What distribution channels and methods are used?
(6) What are the price structures for the product at each level in the distribution channel?
(7) What servicing is carried out by the manufacturer, and what by the distributor?
(8) What are the market shares held by the main competitors?

Exhibit 2.2 Typical market research questions

In addition to official and authoritative figures there are many journals and magazines published on a wide range of topics. The librarian will be able to supply a list of them, together with their publishers' addresses and telephone and fax numbers. You'll find that, whatever business you're in, there will be a publication on it.

All of the professional, technical and trade magazines publish data on their industry. If you wished to investigate even deeper, you could arrange to visit their offices and discuss your proposals. We shall look at the use of these publications for advertising in chapter 6.

One annual publication worthy of mention is the *Marketing Pocket Book*, which is published at around £12 by NTC Publications Ltd of Henley-on-Thames (tel. (0491) 574671). Compiled from official and authoritative sources, it provides an annual summary of all the salient data on the UK market in a convenient form, and is an invaluable guide to the small business person.

A list of further sources of information is given in the Appendix.

Industrial buyers

If you are going to sell to industrial organizations, you should find out what authority the buyer has. The importance of buying varies greatly in companies. It may be little more than a rubber stamp placed on a requisition order raised by the technical people, or it may be a crucial activity in the company, with highly qualified staff having considerable power.

In many companies buying is diffused and involves different people who have varying degrees of influence. The number of buying influences in companies can be up to six or more; only a tiny proportion have just one person concerned with buying. Even the one-man business often has a wife in the background exerting some influence! Over 85 per cent of companies have buying influences of two, three and four people. This group of buying influences is called the *decision-making unit*.

The decision-making unit

A company's decision-making unit is a formal or informal group of people who influence where orders are placed. You may find that you have to sell to more than one person in a company; in effect you have to sell to a group of buying influencers. It will be in your interests to learn a little about modern purchasing techniques.

An important activity in industrial buying is the selection and evaluation of suppliers. Buyers and buying influencers get their knowledge about sources of supply from:

- experience;
- associates;

- people who call on them;
- catalogues;
- trade directories;
- trade advertising and publications;
- exhibitions;
- quotations from potential suppliers.

The evaluation of potential suppliers is made on such criteria as:

- quality;
- initial price;
- operating costs;
- the supplier's distribution facilities;
- reliability of deliveries;
- representative visits;
- technical literature;
- service.

Supplier performance evaluation

Anyone wanting to sell products or services is assessed by the potential buyer. In industrial buying situations this is done more professionally than with the purchase of consumer goods. Several formal evaluation methods are employed, of which the most widely used is the *weighted points method*.

Criteria such as quality, delivery, reliability of delivery, service, accuracy of deliveries and invoices etc. are given weights for importance. Individual suppliers are rated on their performance on these criteria, and their ratings are multiplied by the weights. The grand total provides an overall performance figure for the supplier. Exhibit 2.3 illustrates the general method for a number of criteria of which price, delivery and quality are usually considered to be the three most important in the evaluation of performance of suppliers.

If potential business from a particular company is worth while, and you know that they formally evaluate suppliers, ask for a copy of their evaluation form. The fact that you are a small business person 'trying just a little harder' often softens the heart of the most difficult buyer. By concentrating on what the customer regards as important you can focus your marketing effort on their needs.

Product _____		Supplier _____	
		Date evaluated _____	
Criteria	Weight (*W*) (total = 100)	Rating (*R*) (out of 10)	*W* × *R*
Price	18	8	144
Quality	16	7	112
Delivery	14	7	98
Reliability	10	8	80
Service	14	5	70
Emergency supplies	13	3	39
Uniqueness of product	15	6	90
			633

Performance evaluation (*W* × *R*)/10 = <u>63.3%</u>

Exhibit 2.3 Performance evaluation example

Key points

- Demand for your product will depend on the degree of customers' needs, their ability to pay your price, and their willingness to buy.
- Find out all you possibly can about potential customers and competitors.
- Make full use of your local reference library.
- Restrict the area in which you start initial operations.
- Market research will do nothing for you: you have to do the doing.

3

The product

Outline

The product is of crucial importance in a company, but we must avoid letting it become so important that it is to the detriment of marketing. We look at:

- product attributes and benefits
- industrial and consumer products
- advantages of classifying products in different ways
- products must be customer-related
- product/market planning
- product differentiation
- positioning your product in the market
- use and misuse of the product life-cycle
- analysing the product range
- how to eliminate products from the range

What customers buy

Without a product you have nothing to sell. This vital importance of the product has led many a company to become product-oriented or production-oriented. Products and production departments have become so important in these companies that marketing has been relegated to a minor role or even ignored, and subsequently the company has suffered.

The small business has a first-class opportunity to excel in marketing because it can be started on the ground floor. From the word go, a small business can marketing-orient everything it does; that is, all decisions can be taken with the aim of satisfying customers at a profit to the business.

In marketing terms, a product can best be described as a bundle of satisfactions, and may take the form of a commodity, an article, a piece of equipment, or a service, such as hair-dressing, carpet cleaning, gardening etc. Products are bought because they will do something or satisfy some need; products are not bought for themselves alone.

Every product possesses attributes. These include its characteristics, qualities, properties and idiosyncrasies that have been achieved by its design and the materials used in its production, and all the things that combine to make it what it is. Some of the attributes may be unique to the product and give it an advantage over competitive offers.

A product attribute is of interest to a prospective buyer if it is also a benefit. Attributes that are not customer benefits are only of interest to the seller or manufacturer. It is the failure to understand the importance of product benefits that prevents many companies from developing a marketing-oriented approach.

Industrial or consumer products?

You need to make an early assessment of the product you intend to market. Products may be classified broadly as *consumer goods* or *industrial goods*, but many are sold to both consumers and industry. Often the difference is only a question of the number purchased.

A small marketing-oriented computer dealer in Holborn, London, illustrates this point. The company started life many years ago with typewriter servicing. Later, responding to demand, it began to sell a selected range of standard and portable typewriters. From 1980 they moved with the market trend into the high technology world of the electronic office. They marketed first one machine, and then a range of word processors, personal computers, office machines and peripheral equipment. From 1987 they narrowed their product range, discarding some of the equipment they considered to be attribute-designed rather than benefit-designed, and concentrated on what has come to be known as 'user-friendly' machines.

They sell to individuals, public and private companies, educational and local government departments: the equipment and machines are the same whoever buys. The question of whether they are selling consumer or industrial products is of little consequence.

When they sell a personal computer with a word processing program to an individual it is a consumer product. When they sell six identical packages to a secondary school for use by pupils, or a network of the same equipment to a multinational company with its head office in the home counties, that same product has become an industrial good.

You may start your business marketing products to consumers and find later on that you are able to supply industry. Alternatively you may set out to supply industry with a product or service and subsequently also supply consumers.

Consumer products

Products that are bought by the man in the street, or with the family at weekends, are usually regarded as consumer products, but the buying of such products varies. They may be purchased frequently or infrequently. Some, such as a packet of cereal, cigarettes, matches, or shoe polish, are bought when needed, or when convenient. If they are 'need' products they are called *staple goods*; if not, they are described as *convenience goods*. Some are bought on the spur of the moment: these are *impulse goods*. Others require considerable deliberation before purchase, and involve shopping expeditions: these include washing machines, lawn mowers, suits, dresses etc. Such products are called *shopping goods* or *speciality goods*. Depending on their nature, consumer products may also be described as *durable* or *non-durable* products.

All these consumer product descriptions relate to their general use, degree of need and frequency of purchase. Such classifications are useful in indicating how the product might be marketed. Obviously, an impulse product should be displayed where it can be seen, is likely to be picked up and purchased. This is why displays of confectionery, razor blades, ball-point pens and other impulse goods are near to the check-outs in supermarkets.

Industrial products

Industrial products should also be considered for what they do, rather than for what they are. There are four main categories of industrial products: capital goods; industrial materials; industrial supplies; industrial services.

Industrial capital goods are usually costly items. They include major plant and equipment such as factories, offices, bridges, cranes, fork-lift trucks, machine tools, transport and air conditioning equipment.

Industrial materials are used in the manufacture of other products, and are often changed in shape, form, or formulation. Examples are steel, timber, electrical cable, chemicals and plastic compounds.

Industrial supplies are used up or destroyed in the process of making other products, or are minor items. Examples are fuel, lubricating oil, grinding paste, cutting blades, twist drills, photocopy paper, screws and nails.

Industrial services include everything where no product is supplied, but advice is given or expertise transferred. Examples are management consultancy, technical advice, insurance, cleaning and maintenance.

How to classify products

Classifying your product simply as a consumer or industrial product is inadequate for marketing purposes. Whenever you consider a product, you must also consider its potential market. You may be selling tins of paint and wallpaper; the customer is buying house and room decoration. You could be selling video-recorders; the customer is buying home entertainment. Products and services are bought for what they will do and not for themselves alone. Ensuring that what you are selling is what the customer is buying is a vital prerequisite in marketing.

A businesswoman started a design partnership in 1988, emphasizing that she was able to accept commissions for design work on computer. Her product was in fact, desk-top publishing. This is using a personal computer and laser printer to produce printed material such as reports, booklets, newsletters, sales literature, folders, mailing shots etc. Its advantages over conventional printing are flexibility, speed and lower cost. She soon realized that she had classified her product wrongly for the market.

Desk-top publishing is widely regarded as a second-class printing activity which, though an improvement on duplicated material, can be done in the typing pool. The businesswoman has learned from experience to avoid using the term 'desk-top publishing'; her thriving product is now classified in marketing terms. It is a design service, not computer technology.

The flexibility of desk-top publishing has been exploited by another small businesswoman who markets books for children, not through normal trade channels, but from an airport kiosk. From interested travellers she obtains a dozen or so facts about a child, which are fed into a personal computer. The customer selects one of the available stories, and a few minutes later a personalized book emerges from a laser printer, and is bound ready as a customized gift for the child.

Another small businessman, a chemist, started a specialist chemicals company, but found that the name he chose for it had meaning only for chemists like himself. To his customers, who turned out to be biochemists, the name communicated nothing; they were buying something that the company was apparently not selling. He changed the name of the company to include the word 'Biochem' in the title, and found a more receptive market for the scores of new products he had created.

Make sure that what you are offering for sale is what customers want to buy.

If you were starting an independent travel agency, and wished to market your holiday packages, you wouldn't rent strips of sand and water on a sunny beach somewhere to your customers; you would sell dreams.

Similarly, golfers don't buy more scientifically designed golf clubs; they buy lower scores. The weekend handyman, when buying 10 mm twist drills at his local hardware store, is really buying 10 mm holes. The housewife isn't buying boxes of matches; she's buying boxes of flames.

Company executives are often asked to consider what business they are in, and what business they ought to be in. When the author was lecturing to a group of over seventy Ethiopian Airline executives in Addis Ababa, before starting he asked the delegates to write down what business they thought they were in. With one exception, everyone wrote down 'transportation'. The exception, the manager from New York, had written down 'convenient or delightful destinations'. One must agree; there are better ways of being transported than in a pressurized metal tube 10 km above the earth.

While at times it is true that 'To travel hopefully is a better thing than to arrive', do make sure that, as you are making up your mind what you will be selling in your business, you deal in 'destinations' and not 'transportation'.

The shower-head product

In the previous chapter we classified some consumer and industrial products into suggested market needs, wants and desires. Here is a specific example of product/market planning by a small businessman, a skilled engineer located near Bristol. In 1988 he designed a shower-head that delivers a strong turbo-spray of water at less than half the pressure and flow normally required. It is a clever piece of design, costs about £1, and will fit all existing makes of showers as a replacement head. It has been tested and approved in the UK, the USA, West Germany, France, Denmark and Spain.

It is not a universal need, but is considered to be a new product, and requires considerable effort to sell. Currently the thrust of the marketing effort is to the trade that supplies users. Customers see no immediate benefit in the product when water for showers and baths is freely available. Quite possibly, as UK water rates increase in a privatized industry, a turbo shower-head will become a need product.

The shower-head is both a consumer and an industrial product. It may be sold through retail outlets to users who can replace the head in their existing showers, or to shower manufacturers for inclusion in a range of their products. In Europe the turbo-head might be classified more of a want than a need; in countries where water is scarce it could be classified as a need.

Thus the turbo shower-head is a consumer product; it is an industrial product; it is a want; it is a need. The possible markets for these four classifications are shown in exhibit 3.1.

	Consumer market	Industrial market
Need	Retail outlets in hot countries where water is scarce.	Manufacturers of shower equipment in hot countries.
	Retail outlets in UK areas where water rates are being increased.	European shower manufacturers with export business.
	Mail order selling to DIY enthusiasts in 'water-conscious' areas in UK.	Shower manufacturers in countries where water is expensive.
Want	Retail outlets in holiday areas where people do their repairs and maintenance.	Manufacturers of shower-heads who could use the turbo-head as a product plus in their own marketing efforts.
	Mail order selling to people who are thrifty and appreciate things that save money.	
	Retail outlets in areas with low mains water pressure.	

Exhibit 3.1 Product/market analysis

Sell customers what they need

You may be starting business with a single product. If so, you can concentrate your efforts. Do not be in a hurry to expand your range. More products mean more production runs, larger stocks, more assortments of orders, different customers, different price schedules, more sales literature, more money tied up and so on. Learn to concentrate your efforts, and aim for maximum returns on what you do. One sure way to start going wrong is to develop a product range too early in the life of the business.

Consider the task of knocking a nail into a piece of wood. If you have a light metal hammer that weighs a mere 50 grams or so, with effort you can knock a nail into the wood. But if the hammer head is made of the same weight of expanded polystyrene foam, you can knock the nail for ever: you'll never even get it started into the wood. Your efforts will be dissipated. You will be using the same amount of energy but it will be spread throughout the foam head.

Dissipation of marketing efforts has a similar result. Spread your energies too widely and you'll fail. Concentrate – this is the secret of successful marketing. Once you have found a product or service that you can sell to a market, hammer away at it and become fully conversant with the product, the market, the customers and how to sell it.

Sell customers what they need. No matter how good you think the product is, if the market doesn't need or want it, and cannot be persuaded to appreciate its benefits, it will not sell.

New products

The vast majority of new products are those that do things similar to existing products but in improved or different ways.

Ball-point pens replaced ink pens. Both are used to write with but the ball-point uses a different system. In the office the typewriter replaced the pen. Although both will produce letters and invoices, the typewriter does it more quickly, can produce copies at the same time, and the results are possibly easier to read. Word processors superseded typewriters: the output is similar but produced very much faster, more accurately, and the equipment is able to store data. In their time, steel nib pens, ball-points, typewriters and word processors were new products.

Several generations of calculators have appeared on the market since the abacus was introduced. All can be used to perform various calculations quicker than with pen and paper, but each new product has either increased the speed of computation or has more built-in functions.

Calculating the amount of money you need to start and run your business will be the same whether you do it with an abacus, slide-rule, a solar-powered electronic calculator, personal computer, or paper and pencil.

New products will do similar tasks to those already on the market, but will do them easier, faster and at less cost – that is, with additional *identifiable benefits* to the user. It is not often that a product has to be designed to do something that has never been done before, such as walking on the moon. In general, new products are different ways of doing old things.

Some years ago the garden wheelbarrow was superseded by a new invention – the ball-barrow. The advantages of the large ball instead of the wheel in heavy soil or wet clay made its merits readily understandable. However, not all new products are able to demonstrate their advantages so easily. Even with the advantages obviously understood, gardeners didn't rush out the next day and buy one. Wheelbarrows are a speciality product and very infrequently purchased.

Old products

Old products are not geriatric merchandise but widely known items that have been marketed for a long time. Soap is an old product. Matches are old products; an innovation was the change in the formulation of the head to provide safety matches which ignite only when struck on the strip of material on the side of the matchbox.

Pencils are old products. Two improvements have been made over the years: instead of being round they were made with six flat sides to prevent their rolling so easily off the desk, and a rubber was fitted. Propelling pencils were introduced, although the lead had to be pushed back by hand; then propelling and retractable pencils were made. The latest improvement came around 1975 when a company marketed an automatic-feed pencil; as the lead is used it is automatically fed to the pencil point while writing.

Washing-machine powders are old products, widely known and widely advertised; some might say over-advertised. During 1987 a new product appeared – washing-machine liquids. Instead of tipping a quantity of powder into the washing-machine's container, liquid is poured in, or put into a plastic ball and placed inside the machine with the clothes. The absence of powder residue in and around the container gives the liquid a considerable advantage and, because it mixes with the water more quickly than the powder, it is said to penetrate the washing more easily.

A company launching on to the market another washing powder

or liquid, soap, a pencil, ball-point, new calculator or word processor would not be marketing a new product so much as new type of 'old' product. It is best described as a competitive product.

Analysing your product

You have to decide whether the product or service you intend to market is a new product or a competitive product. If it is a competitive product – that is, competing with the other 'old' products on the market – it will need a very strong selling effort; if it is a 'new' product, it will also need a strong sales and marketing effort, but the direction of the attack is different.

With a competitive product the thrust of your marketing effort will be directed to competition. With a new product the direction is toward potential customers; you have to educate them in the advantages of using it instead of whatever it is they use now.

Products can be grouped into two main types: *standard products* and *non-standard products*. In marketing terminology, standard products are referred to as *non-differentiated* products. This term is of value because non-standard products can then be described as differentiated products. This is bang in line with the argument about product/market planning. A non-standard product can be marketed to appeal to specific market segments or sub-markets. It can be *differentiated*.

You will probably have already decided whether your product is to be marketed as a consumer or industrial product, and judged its degree of need to that market. If the degree of need is high, it is likely to be a standard product, one that cannot be easily differentiated from its competitors.

With standard products such as nails, screws, electrical cable, insulations, copper piping, plastic sheeting, tubing, ball-cock valves, door fittings, hinges etc. there are often industry specifications to ensure that they are more or less identical. If you intend to market a standard product – that is, one that cannot be differentiated – you will need to comply with the appropriate specification.

If yours is a non-essential product, you may need to differentiate it. Perhaps you can make it look different or operate in a different way from competitors' products, perhaps it can be made easier to use or given some distinctive characteristics to set it apart from the competition.

Standard products

Because standard products cannot be easily differentiated from one another they are often sold on price. But price cutting of standard products depresses profits very quickly unless you can produce at a much lower cost than your competitors.

One small businessman did just this; Mr Karsanbhai Patel, in India. And he did it against the giant multinational, Lever Bros. In the 1970s they were the market leader in India for detergents, dominating the market with Surf. By maintaining the right combinations of performance, price and presentation they had kept the product firmly in consumers' minds as the standard by which to judge all other powders.

Mr Patel decided that Surf, although a high-quality product, was also a high-priced product, and that a potential market existed for a low-priced one. He decided to market a competitive low-priced product. To do this he had to ensure that his costs would be low enough to combat the inevitable counter-attacks.

He adapted his manufacturing methods to Indian conditions, with a chain of workshops in which people mixed the ingredients by hand. His low-priced Nirma brand outsold the Lever product by about three to one. In 1987 his turnover exceeded £150m, and he intends to double that by 1990.

As a new, small business he had some tax advantages, but his labour costs were about one-fifth of Hindustan Lever's costs, and his work-force was non-unionized. His overheads were low, with about 200 supervisors looking after a work-force of some 10,000. He is no longer a small businessman.

If you intended to start a business with a standard product, you would need to produce it, as did Mr Patel, at a much lower cost than competitors, otherwise it would be a recipe for disaster.

Differentiation does not exist in the product's characteristics, but in the intangible factors that are promoted by marketing. In other words, differentiation is not a product attribute, but a measured distinction in the buyer's mind. Many standard products are successfully marketed with a degree of product differentiation by changing some of the other marketing mix components: petrol, washing powders, light bulbs, envelopes and stationery are common examples. However, such differentiation requires immense inputs of money and resources, and there may be another Mr Patel lurking round the corner!

Normally for a small business to compete with a standard product it is necessary to concentrate on a small segment of the market with perhaps the advantages of local appeal. Jams, honey, pickles, preserves and similar foodstuffs are standard products, yet some small businesses have been built up with differentiated products capitalizing on local characteristics.

Standard products are not potentially fruitful areas for the small business. Ask yourself about your product:

- Is it a true standard product with an authoritative specification?
- Does its use show a cost-saving to customers?
- Are there many competitors in the market?
- Can it be produced at a significantly lower unit cost than competitive products?
- Can it be marketed in a different way that will make it stand out from the competition?
- Is it possible to concentrate on a small part of the market and achieve an advantage over the competition?

If your product is a true standard product with a widely accepted specification, unless your answers to these questions favour your proposition and you have potentially powerful advantages over existing competitors, you had better forget it and look for something else.

Cost-saving products

Your product may be a standard product, but when in use it shows a significant cost-saving or has other benefits for customers. If so, can the saving or benefit be translated into money terms?

If you have been in business for some time, it would be a simple matter to obtain data from customers and use cost-saving information as sales points. If you are just starting your business, you will need an independent evaluation of your product to support your cost-saving contentions. As you obtain sales you use customers' experience – with their permission of course – in your sales and advertising claims.

You would need to demonstrate that the cost-saving or benefit your product can offer is significant; the degree of significance will depend on the product, and it may be a few pence or many pounds.

A small computer-aided design (CAD) business was started in Berkshire in 1987, and one of the standard programs offered was for the planning and management of facilities. A company's facilities are coming under greater scrutiny because of its escalating costs. Cost of space, especially in city centres is horrendous, and its economic use is often crucial to the success of a company. The siting of office furniture, machines and equipment, the storing of supplies, and the consideration of the traffic of people having to move between different departments in the course of their normal daily work all require careful planning. Carrying out such a task of allocating space, resources, furniture and people to a multi-storey block to minimize costs is comparatively easy with a computer-aided design program.

The Berkshire company obtained independent opinions and assessments from various associations and architects by supplying their program at no cost. With the few initial appraisals, they succeeded in landing their first orders for the CAD program. Now, as soon as customers have notable results, a case study is prepared, often by the customer. These are then used as persuasive literature with potential customers.

Lower-cost products

Many researches have demonstrated that buyers are reluctant to move from their present suppliers for a price advantage of less than 10 per cent. This is, of course, a general finding; decisions on some high volume purchases often turn on fractions of a penny. The vast majority of ordinary everyday products are repeat-purchased by companies from the same two or three sources; buyers do not like changing suppliers unless they have very strong reasons.

You may be able to produce a product at a significantly lower unit cost than your competitors, but this is a danger area. Small businesses frequently start out with the product being made in the garage, or back room, with the invoices and accounts prepared on the dining table after dinner; costs are naturally low. While this is a perfectly acceptable way of starting a small business, the prices to customers must not be related to costs, but to prices in the market.

As a small business with low overheads, you should be able to make things at much lower costs that competitors operating from factories and offices. But you will be unable to expand the business beyond a certain size without incurring greater expense.

You have two main lines of attack. Either sell at a low price, make a little profit on a low turnover, and treat the business as a side-line, or sell at prices comparable with those in the market, using the extra profit for promotion and future business expansion.

Non-standard products

A truly non-standard product, one that can be readily differentiated from its competitors, is unlikely to be a need product unless it is highly protected legally with patents. Even then, need products are subject to intensive research for substitutes and few remain in profitable isolation for long.

The Polaroid camera is a highly differentiated product. For estate agents requiring quick photographs of property, photographers needing an quick photo of a complicated studio set before taking the larger shots, or for rapid passport pictures, the Polaroid is a need product. It was protected with patents, but this did not stop Eastman Kodak from eventually entering the market with their version of an 'instant picture' camera. However, after many years of argument and a two-year legal wrangle, Kodak were forced by the courts to withdraw their camera and pay around $250 million in compensation to the 16.5 million holders of the useless camera.

You can estimate how 'non-standard' your product is, how different from others available on the market, and its likely degree of need, by what is known as *positioning*.

Product positioning

A product's position in the market is its total image, and its reputation compared with other products. Often there is a 'best' product, universally acclaimed by the market as such. The image may be strong, relatively obscure, or a complex mix of apparently unrelated beliefs. The varying images for some products prove that product differentiation is a distinction in the buyer's mind and not in the product itself.

A product's position is determined by the strength of the market's perception and preference for it compared with competitive products, but one attribute is more important than the others – its price.

Customers make the initial assumption that price reflects quality. Therefore the simplest way to position a product is to list all competitive products in descending order of price. Thus with four products, A, B, C, D, and your product, Y, they could be listed as in exhibit 3.2.

Products	Price
A	£90.00
C	£85.00
Y	£83.00
D	£73.00
B	£67.50

Exhibit 3.2 Positioning products by price

This might be as far as you are prepared to go; you have positioned your product and see that it occupies a place neatly in the middle of its competitors. To explore further, consider the differences between the products' prices, not simply their order. The price differences vary from £2 between your product and C, to £10 between your product and D. If these are shown on a simple scale as in exhibit 3.3, they give a more pictorial representation of the products' positions.

Products		Price
A	–	£90.00
	–	
	–	
	–	
	–	
C	–	£85.00
	–	
Y	–	£83.00
	–	
	–	
	–	
	–	
	–	
	–	
	–	
D	–	£73.00
	–	
	–	
	–	
B	–	£68.00

Exhibit 3.3 Ranking and scaling products

Your product should have much better attributes and benefits than D, and your main competitor is likely to be C. You should compare C with your product in some detail. If your product offers advantages over C, your price advantage of £2 will be seen by the market to be greater than this.

Another method widely used to compare products with competition is illustrated in exhibit 3.4. Competing products are listed in the first column and *key benefits* (not attributes) in the other columns. Products that possess the benefits have the appropriate cells marked.

Product	Easy to use	Versatile	Fast action	Easily up-graded	Low price
A	\	\	\	\	
B	\	\	\		\
C	\	\		\	
D			\		\
E	\				\
F		\	\	\	

Exhibit 3.4 Analysis of product benefits

The product life-cycle

Most products have a similar life pattern to human beings: they are born, grow, mature and die. However, it is necessary to distinguish between individual products, and groups of products or product lines. Salt, whisky, bread, shoes and umbrellas are examples of product groups that are unlikely to die. But individual brands and manufactures of these often follow a typical life-cycle pattern: introduction, growth, maturity, decline.

Although several different shapes have been identified, most products exhibit slow growth during their introduction, then rapid growth, a period of stability, and then decline. Apart from the occasional idiosyncratic shape of a product life-cycle, the main difficulty in using it as a planning guide is that we do not know how long it will be from the end of the growth stage to the start of the decline stage. Decline could be a month or two away; it could be many years. Only with some hi-tech products where product development generally is widely known can life-cycles be estimated with any degree of accuracy. Some fad products have a rapid, almost violent growth stage, and then fall away and decline just as suddenly. The graph is shaped more like a pyramid. Consider hula-hoops, skate-boards, computer games etc.

The value in estimating which particular stage a product has reached is that it indicates what marketing tactics could be employed. Some of these are suggested for product, price, place, promotion and service in the typical S-shaped product life-cycle illustrated in exhibit 3.5.

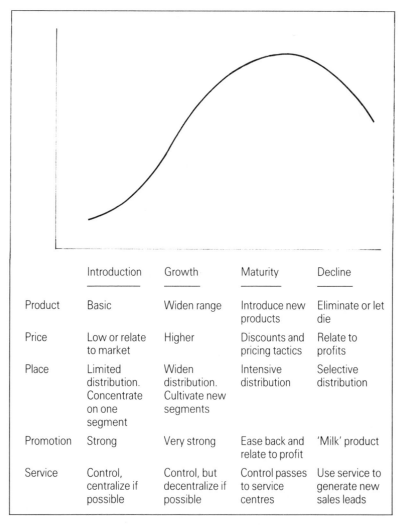

	Introduction	Growth	Maturity	Decline
Product	Basic	Widen range	Introduce new products	Eliminate or let die
Price	Low or relate to market	Higher	Discounts and pricing tactics	Relate to profits
Place	Limited distribution. Concentrate on one segment	Widen distribution. Cultivate new segments	Intensive distribution	Selective distribution
Promotion	Strong	Very strong	Ease back and relate to profit	'Milk' product
Service	Control, centralize if possible	Control, but decentralize if possible	Control passes to service centres	Use service to generate new sales leads

Exhibit 3.5 Product life-cycle tactics

In general, you should not enter a market with a product in its decline stage. Estimating the particular stage of a product is a useful exercise. Here are some examples:

aluminium sheeting	maturity
bicycle	regenerated growth
black-and-white TV	decline
bricks for building	maturity
children's bricks	maturity
colour TV	late growth
cotton-weaving machines	decline
electric fan-heaters	maturity to decline
electric radiant-heaters	decline
electric typewriters	decline
electronic typewriters	maturity to decline
electronic toys	growth
farm tractors	maturity
gas fires	decline
intruder alarms	rapid growth
minicomputers	rapid growth
motor cars	maturity
personal transceivers	late growth
plastic hose-pipe	maturity
rubber floor tiles	decline
steel girders	maturity
word processors	growth

You may not agree with all the suggested stages because we are living in a world of unprecedented uncertainty. Bicycles, for example, were in the decline stage early in the 1980s, but are now experiencing a new growth stage.

Product range analysis

If you have more than one product, you should know which ones provide the turnover and which the profit. Use a form similar to that in exhibit 3.6. List the products in descending order of turnover. Insert the cumulative turnover percentage in the final column as you insert successive turnover figures.

Use a modified version of the form for product profits. When both have been completed, you can see if the products that provide the bulk of your sales turnover also provide the same proportion of profit.

	Product	Sales value	% of turnover	Cumulative %
1.				
2.				
3.				
4.				
5.				
6.				

Exhibit 3.6 Analysis of product turnover

The so-called *pareto* principle is often evident, with 80 per cent of the turnover coming from 20 per cent of the products. This principle was suggested by Vilfredo Pareto (1848–1923) an Italian sociologist and economist, who observed a general tendency of approximately 80 per cent of effects to arise from 20 per cent of causes.

Product modification and elimination

Sooner or later, you will have to modify, change, improve, or remove a product from your range. As with initial planning, don't do this in isolation. Consider the product/market. Five questions have to be answered:

- Does the present product range need to be changed?
- Irrespective of whether the product range is to be changed, should current market segments be changed?
- Irrespective of other changes, should the current marketing mix be changed?
- If the product range is to be changed, should this be by product modification, re-positioning, elimination, and/or introduction of a new product?
- If new market segments and/or new products are to be introduced, should this be done ourselves, or by joining with another company?

If you are in business on your own, you will have to form a committee of one! If you have responsible people working with you, use them in your deliberations. Aim to quantify the criteria you use to come to decisions, and, if it is possible, adopt a formal appraisal method.

First, decide the criteria relevant to your business, then give weights to each. The weightings are the same for all products but should be reviewed every six months or so. Individual products are rated for the criteria and multiplied by the appropriate weighting.

Product _____

Date assessed _____

	Weight (W)	Rating (R)		W × R
1. Product contributes a high percentage of total profit.	10	1 Low	10 High	____
2. Product contributes a high percentage of total sales turnover.	9	1 Low	10 High	____
3. Product in decline stage.	8	1 Yes	10 No	____
4. Product difficult to make.	7	1 No	10 Yes	____
5. Product in maturity stage.	6	1 Yes	10 No	____
6. If product dropped, facilities released for other work.	5	1 Yes	10 No	____
7. Competitors cutting prices.	5	1 Often	10 Seldom	____
8. Competition is increasing.	4	1 Strong	10 Weak	____
9. Rounds out a group of products.	3	1 No	10 Yes	____
10. A lot of capital has been invested in the product in recent years.	3	1 Not much	10 A lot	____
			Total W × R	____

Exhibit 3.7 Specimen product elimination chart

All the 'rated weights' are added to give a total. For convenience, make the weights add to a round number. In the specimen product elimination chart shown in exhibit 3.7, the weights add to 60. Therefore the maximum total is 600.

A product that receives an overall low rating is a candidate for removal. You or the committee will decide what criteria are to be used, and how low is a low rating. In this example, which has been edited from the records of a small engineering company in Warwick, any product with a rating less than 300 is considered for possible improvement, those rated less than 150 are candidates for elimination. They are not automatically removed from the range but are subject to intensive analysis to determine what is the likely effect on profits, and customers if they are so removed.

Key points

- Customers buy products for what they will do, not for what they are.
- Classify your products in terms of degree of need to target customers.
- Plan products for specific markets.
- Sell product benefits, not attributes.
- Don't dissipate your energy and marketing resources; concentrate your efforts.

4

The price

Outline

Pricing is important: sound pricing policy generates profits and keeps the company in business. We look at:

- the dangers of pricing too high and too low
- the two main pricing strategies
- how to develop a standard mark-up
- business expansion and pricing procedures
- influences on the price level
- high- and low-price policies
- the use of discounts
- preparing a price list
- the importance of controlling the credit given

The purpose of price

The purpose of setting a price on your product or service is to sell it and make a profit. Often you will need a fine sense of judgment to avoid its being too high or too low.

If you start a gardening service, as you try to get business, people will ask the price of your service. Set it too high, and they will not be interested. Set it too low, and they'll think you don't have sufficient skill and experience of gardening. The price you ask establishes the quality of your product or service in the minds of customers, and helps to establish its position in the market.

You can understand how pricing too high can create dissatisfaction in customers; what is not always understood is how pricing too low can create dissatisfaction.

If your product requires back-up or some other service, especially after-sales service, then if you set the price too low, you may not have sufficient margin in the price to look after your customers. They become disenchanted with the product, the service and with you.

Pricing is one of your more difficult tasks. No one really enjoys doing it, yet it determines the volume of business you achieve: your total sales, revenue and profit.

From the start of your business adopt a system that enables you to price a product or service quickly. This will minimize the amount of time you spend in the future on pricing problems, and will avoid your having to make arbitrary decisions.

All decisions you make regarding the product – its production, packaging, storage, distribution, promotion and service – will affect the price. Therefore the pricing system you adopt should include consideration of all factors likely to affect price.

Price and profit

Profit and price are linked. The higher the price, the greater the profit; the lower the price, the lower the profit. But it is usually easier to sell the lower-priced product or service. You need to determine the relationship between your product's price, or fee for a service, and the number of units or services you are likely to sell.

There are two main ways in which you can price your product: work up from the cost of making and selling; work down from what the market will pay. The former is called *cost-pricing*, the latter is *value-pricing*.

Cost-pricing

The popularity of cost-pricing is its simplicity. You determine the cost of making, buying-in, or supplying the product or service, and then add costs for other activities and profit. The result is the price.

Retailing of consumer products is a typical situation for cost-pricing. To the cost of buying items is added a percentage to cover other costs and profit (plus the appropriate percentage for VAT if applicable): this establishes the retail price.

The particular percentage added to the bought-in price is related to the average speed of sales of the product. This speed of sales is called *stock-turn*. The higher your stock-turn, that is, the more times you sell the average stock you hold, the lower the percentage profit. If you sell highly perishable goods, you probably turn over your stock two or three times a week. Retail mark-up on such things as fish, vegetables etc. is low, but you make this low percentage a lot of times because of the high stock-turn.

A product with a low stock-turn carries a higher percentage mark-up. You make more money, but you make it less often. Furniture, which is purchased infrequently, has a high mark-up of 45 or 50 per cent. Jewellery has an even higher mark-up.

Cost-pricing of industrial products is sometimes crude, with one or two percentages added to get the net-of-tax price. In some companies it is highly developed, with purchasing, manufacturing and marketing activities analysed and percentage oncosts established for each.

Developing a standard mark-up

If it is appropriate for your product, and you plan to adopt a cost-plus procedure, you should develop a standard mark-up. You collect all the cost data about your product or service, then calculate a simple percentage oncost to your basic cost to arrive at a price.

A butterfly farm invited the author to advise them on their marketing in general and to devise a pricing system that could be applied to all their products. They obtain moths and butterflies from all over the world, and set and arrange them in display boxes, which are sold as decorations. Customers can choose from several sizes of made-up display boxes, or order a box with their own choice of butterflies and moths.

Many orders were received for individual boxes with a variety of different contents being specified. As some of the more colourful moths and butterflies are rare and costly, pricing was a burdensome task. The method used by the owner was to base price on cost, adding a sufficient margin to cover overheads, selling expenses and profit. But this exercise was carried out for every individual box!

The cost of the different sizes of boxes was fixed; the contents varied. Therefore the price of the completed display box depended on the contents. The farm's annual overheads, administration, selling and delivery costs were established, and the average number of sales of display boxes was determined. From these calculations the pricing formula adopted for the display boxes was the cost of the box plus three times the cost of the contents.

With their list of butterfly and moth costs they could easily price any display box. Even on the phone, with the customer describing the size of box and general colour scheme desired, it was a simple matter to quote a price.

An industrial product mark-up

A tiny industrial business in the Midlands had a simple pricing procedure when it started out with one product. As the company progressed, and more products were added to the range, the pricing system became inadequate and resulted in lost sales and falling profits.

All costs and overheads had been calculated, and to arrive at a price a standard mark-up of 60 per cent was applied to the cost of raw materials and direct labour. This 60 per cent oncost was sufficient for all other costs and profit. Thus a product with £30 of raw materials and £10 labour – a total cost of £40 – was priced at £40 plus 60 per cent (£24) to make £64. This calculation is set out in exhibit 4.1.

A more accurate method of pricing was needed to keep a check on costs and profit, and to price more keenly against competitors. It

	Product A
Cost of materials	£30.00
Cost of labour	£10.00
Total cost	£40.00
Oncost 60%	£24.00
Price	£64.00

Exhibit 4.1 Cost-pricing an industrial product

was decided to keep the cost-plus method, but to break down the percentage oncost and get at the true costs for the increasingly varied manufacturing process.

The root of the problem was that 60 per cent for both materials and labour was being added when, in fact, these two items varied for different products.

After an analysis of costs for a range of products, it was agreed that, instead of the 60 per cent oncost on materials and labour, 25 per cent of the materials cost and 75 per cent of the labour cost should be added to establish the price.

The effect of this change can be seen in exhibit 4.2, where the new price is compared with the previous price for product A, and for three other products. Note that where the labour content is low compared with the materials content, the price is substantially less with the new costing procedure.

| | Product A | | Product B | | Product C | | Product D | |
	£ Old	£ New	£ Old	£ New	£ Old	£ New	£ Old	£ New
Materials	30.00	30.00	5.00	5.00	20.00	20.00	40.00	40.00
Labour	10.00	10.00	35.00	35.00	20.00	20,00	5.00	5.00
Total cost	40.00	40.00	40.00	40.00	40.00	40.00	45.00	45.00
Oncosts	24.00		24.00		24.00		27.00	
Materials 25%		7.50		1.25		5.00		10.00
Labour 75%		7.50		26.25		15.00		3.75
Price	£64.00	£55.00	£64.00	£67.50	£64.00	£60.00	£72.00	£58.75

Exhibit 4.2 Old and new cost-pricing methods

Using a costing sheet for pricing

The company discussed above now employs over twenty people. The costing sheet for pricing which it uses has been edited and illustrated in exhibit 4.3. Suitably modified, it may be appropriate for your business. Let us look at each of the sections.

```
                        PRICING SHEET

Product _____       Date _____

                                    £              £

Cost of materials                  ___·___
Items purchased                    ___·___
Storage                            ___·___
                                                   ___·___
Labour                             ___·___
                                                   ___·___
Stock room                         ___·___
                                                   ___·___
Administration costs               ___·___
Management                         ___·___
Sales costs                        ___·___
Advertising                        ___·___
Contingencies                      ___·___
                                                   ___·___
                              Profit 25%           ___·___
                              Price                ___·___
```

Exhibit 4.3 Specimen pricing sheet

Cost of materials

The actual cost of materials for the production of one unit is inserted. If there are several product sizes, a pricing sheet is completed for each one. Suppose you were making garden furniture and had three different tables. The quantity and type of materials used might be different for each table. Wastage and off-cuts would also be included in the cost of materials.

Items purchased

Many components, such as handles, hinges, plastic fittings, screws, glass etc. are bought in. The cost of these is inserted for the particular product being priced.

Storage

Storing raw materials, components, accessories and bought-in items takes up space. The space occupied by the materials has to be recovered in the price of the product. To calculate the exact volume occupied by the materials used in one product would be tiresome and unrealistic; you need to calculate total cost of storage, and average over the products.

A problem that often arises is that more than one product is made, and they are made in different sizes. During the course of a year or so the pattern of your sales may change, and you may be selling more of a large-sized product than the small size. If you averaged the cost of space over all products, your costing may need revising. This problem will only be serious if the cost of storage is high.

Labour

The cost of labour in producing a product needs to be accurately calculated. Problems arise when the small business starts to grow, and you employ people to help you make your product. People do not work at the same rate or at the same standard. If you based the cost of labour to make your product on your own efforts, you may find that, because it is your business and your interest, your labour efforts may not be duplicated by employees. Also some employees work faster than others. Without becoming involved in labour rates, standard times, standard costs and other work-study practices, make sure that the cost of labour required to produce the product that is inserted in the pricing sheet reflects what actually happens in practice.

Stock room

Not only do raw materials need to be stored, finished products need to be held until they are sold. The cost of space for storing finished goods is usually higher than for raw materials because better surroundings are expected and, in addition, more space is needed. Finished products take up more space than the raw materials and components from which they are made.

Avoid getting into complex calculations. Establish the annual cost of finished goods space, and average over the number of products approximate to the space they occupy.

Administration costs

Early in a new small business much of the general administration is done by the owner and family. As the business develops, other people have to do this work – and be paid for it. From the start a realistic replacement charge should be included for work done in connection with the business. If you are working in the evenings, writing letters, filing papers, keeping your books in order etc., the costs of doing this tend to be overlooked. When someone has to be employed to do these tasks you can keep costs down by employing part-time people; but if you do, you should ensure that what is entered in your pricing sheet reflects the true cost of employing a full-time person and paying for social security, holiday pay etc. If you fail to do this, when you expand the business your costs escalate and erode profits.

Management

Management of a business should be regarded as separate from owning and directing it. When you start, you will be the owner and, most likely, the manager, the worker, the clerk, the telephone operator and probably make tea and coffee for the staff as well!

If you start a small hotel, as the owner, the buck stops with you. You will frequently find yourself having to do jobs such as making the beds, cleaning the rooms, cooking breakfast, refuelling the boiler etc. All this and managing it too!

As you become successful, you will hire help; if you are very successful, you will hire managers. The position is the same as with administrative costs: include the cost of management in the price structure from the start of your business, otherwise when you reach a size that requires you to employ management, your costs take a sudden, unprofitable jump.

Sales costs

There is always the small matter of selling. Apart from having to make the product in your early stages, you'll have to do the paperwork, deal with the multitude of forms required by officialdom, manage the business and sell the products. If you don't sell your product or service, you make no money.

Don't ignore selling and the costs of selling. Initially you will do it yourself. Charge realistic costs in the pricing sheet. If you are starting in the hi-tech area, especially in anything to do with computers, when you want to hire an ordinary sales person, the costs will horrify you.

Advertising

An oncost is included in the price for advertising. We shall deal with this subject in chapter 6. For the pricing sheet, you could insert a percentage of the price of the product. But this creates a problem. You are attempting to do this before you have arrived at the price, which includes an oncost for advertising, which is based on the price, which includes an oncost . . . You can see the circular reasoning! So until you have refined your procedures, you could insert, say, 5 per cent of the total cost of materials and labour.

Contingencies

In any form designed to account for costs, it is advisable to have a line for contingencies to allow for changes not covered under other headings.

Cost-plus dangers

While the cost-plus method of pricing is easy to adopt, use it when your activities are simple. As they develop and become more complex, adopt a regular procedure of updating percentage oncosts along the lines of the example quoted above.

Arguments against the use of a standard mark-up procedure are that there are no periodic appraisals of market and economic conditions, and, when you employ people, the method offers no stimulus to efficiency. It's easy to become accustomed to a fixed mark-up: costs that might otherwise be investigated are accepted because it is assumed that the mark-up covers them.

If you persist in cost-pricing long after you should have become more sophisticated, competitors will soon spot opportunities for differential pricing. You would find that you were being beaten on price too often.

A more important argument against the cost-plus method is that it is concerned with the supply side of activities, not the demand side. Demand for your product creates sales; sales generate profit. If the pricing method ignores demand, you could be losing sales because your prices are too high, or losing the opportunity of more profit because your prices are too low.

However, if your new business is in a distribution channel as a middleman, buying from manufacturers and selling to retailers, cost-pricing is normal. The manufacturers whose products you handle usually take the responsibility for establishing recommended retail prices.

Value-pricing

Value-pricing is setting the price at what the customer will pay. Unfortunately, customers seldom tell you what they are prepared to pay: it is the seller who has to name the price.

If you have ever advertised an item for sale in the classified columns of a publication, you'll appreciate the difficulty of setting the price. If you have ever sold your house, you will have been advised to state a high price and be prepared to drop it.

In business, you don't always get the opportunity of bargaining with the potential customer. You are asked, 'How much?'

Your guide is the price of comparable products and services, but ensure that they are comparable. If you are selling a product, look at prices of similar products in shops, departmental stores, cash-and-carry operators, discount houses, mail-order catalogues and any other outlet you find. Inspect the goods if you can: look at the materials used and the standard of manufacture. There is a lot of truth in the saying, 'You get what you pay for'. Compare a low-priced holdall with one many times the price. The higher price is usually justified by the better quality of materials, superior construction, better locking arrangement and a more robust method of securing handle and straps.

It is better to charge a high price and give a discount than to set a net price. Furthermore, if trade practice is to set prices at a few pence below a round figure (e.g. £14.95 or £3.99), follow that practice. The dilemma in value-pricing is that the price has to be set at what the customer will pay, but *you* have to set it. Whatever level you set, it does *not* mean that you will sell at that price.

If you construct a price by working upwards from cost to what you think the customer will pay, you enter an important area of pricing.

Price affects demand: set it too high and you won't sell many; set it too low and you'll sell a lot but at a small profit – possibly at a loss. What is more important is the effect on demand of a change in price. If price is lowered by, say, 10 per cent, will demand be increased by 10 per cent? Or more, or less, than 10 per cent?

The way in which demand is affected by price changes is called the *elasticity of demand*. If, say, a 10 per cent price reduction causes sales to increase more than 10 per cent, demand is elastic.

The general relationship is this: for any proportionate change in price, if sales change proportionately more, demand is elastic; if they change less than the price change, demand is inelastic.

Supposing you sold 1,000 of your product at £5, and decided to lower the price by 15 per cent to £4.25. If you then sold, say, 20 per cent more (i.e. 1,200), demand for your product is elastic.

Consider the situation shown in exhibit 4.4. By lowering the price, sales have been increased. Price was reduced by 28.5 per cent (from £14 to £10), but sales increased by only 25 per cent (15 as a

Price	Sales
£14	60
£10	75

Exhibit 4.4 Demand and price changes

percentage of 60). Sales increased by a smaller percentage than the percentage change in price: the product has an inelastic demand.

This is not contrived, but has great significance for your pricing policy. First, although sales have increased by lowering the price, turnover has fallen. At £14, turnover is £840; at £10, it is £750.

There is worse to come. Supposing there is a fixed cost of £400, and each product cost £4 to make. Sales have increased; however, not only has turnover gone down, but profit has fallen drastically. The situation is shown in exhibit 4.5.

Price	Sales	Turnover	Fixed cost (£400)	Variable cost (£4)	Total cost	Profit
£14	60	£840	£400	£240	£640	£200
£10	75	£750	£400	£300	£700	£50

Exhibit 4.5 An inelastic product

If you are just starting your business, you have no sales records to analyse for likely demand elasticity. As you make sales, pay particular attention to the sensitivity of price. Sometimes, with a highly elastic product, a small change in price makes a world of difference to sales.

Pricing objectives

A *pricing objective* is simply what you intend to achieve by the price you set for various products and services. The objective can be long-term or short-term. An objective must not be too general, liable to conflict with others, be over-ambitious, or ignore competition. Your pricing objectives should relate to your position in the market and your financial resources. Above all, objectives must be attainable, able to be measured and realistic.

You may think of adopting as a long-term pricing objective the *maximization of profit*. This is not an objective, but an aim or intention. An objective has to measurable: how do you decide when you have maximized profit? If you aim to get as much profit as possible in the short term, you will attract competitors into the market. Competition constrains profit maximization.

It is better to decide on the total profit you hope to achieve in the long run, calculate prices accordingly and monitor sales.

Your pricing problem

You can adopt a high-price policy or a low-price policy. Both have their merits. At one extreme the price could be ceiling-price or value-price, which is the worth of the product in money terms as seen by the customer: it is what the market will pay. The other extreme is the floor-price or cost-price, and is the lowest price computed from costs of production and selling. If you sell at cost-price, you cover all costs but make no profit.

Your problem is to set the price somewhere between the floor and the ceiling and, as was discussed in the introduction to this chapter, the price has to be attractive enough for buyers to buy, and sufficient for profits to be made. Several influences affect the level you choose.

Influence of value

The influence of value is probably the most powerful of these influences. Consider the value of your product to satisfy a need. You can influence the potential buyer in three ways:

- give the product more value;
- educate the buyer on its value by publicity;
- adjust the price to fit the product's existing value.

Estimate your product's value by *value analysis* – a comparison of its benefits with those of competitive products.

The value of a technical product can often be determined by measuring the savings made through its use. Be rigorous in your appraisal; personal judgment can distort what is otherwise a sound approach to setting a price.

Influence of cost

The influence of cost plus a little profit establishes the floor-price. Pricing at levels near the floor is easy; all the costs and expenses are known, and an acceptable profit can be added. However, potential buyers will not always pay what it costs to make a product, and many products fail because the market values them less than their cost of production and distribution.

Influence of competition

Competition greatly influences price setting. You can encourage competition by setting a high price, or discourage it with a low one. If your product requires special knowledge or is not easy to make, a low price will not encourage competitors. If you set a high price, this might make it worth while for others to have a go.

Influence of promotion

Price must include an amount to cover promotion. If you are starting a business with a new product, especially if competition is strong, your publicity will have to cross a *threshold of perception* before customers are aware of your product. It may be necessary to allocate a special fund to cope with this task, but, in the long run, all promotional funds must come from sales.

Influence of distribution method

How you distribute your product will influence its price. The closer you get to the user, the more costly is distribution. If you supply direct to the user, each sale is a separate transaction, and although you pocket the profits that would normally be taken by middlemen your costs are much higher. The advantage of getting closer to the user is that you retain greater control over selling and marketing activities.

If you supply to a large retailer or a wholesaler, you have the advantage of selling in dozens rather than ones, but you lose control over sales and marketing.

Good marketing can be simplified: getting the right goods, at the right price, in the right place, at the right time. If your product is not in the market at the right time, your sales will suffer. But if it's not in the right place, you won't sell any at all.

Distribution is vital to your success: if your product is not available at convenient outlets for customers, you'll sell none. In chapter 3 you read that the product is the most important factor in marketing; distribution is the next most important. This will be looked at in detail in chapter 5.

Customers cannot always buy products that fit their needs exactly; they make compromises for quality, weight, size, price, performance, colour etc. Irrespective of the allowances they are prepared to make, if the product is not there, no compromise can be made: there will be no sales. Even if your prices are the lowest in the market, no amount of advertising can overcome inadequate or inept distribution.

To find competent distributors who will sell your product aggressively costs money. They expect to receive their earnings for holding and distributing stocks immediately the product is sold. This sum must be contained in the price, and must match the margins received from competitors.

Influence of public opinion

People usually have a fair idea of the price of a product, whether it is a consumer or an industrial product: a tube of toothpaste, a fork-lift truck, a bar of soap, a motor-car tyre, a ball-point pen, an office desk, a garden chair, a clothes line, a word processor etc. When buying a product, they will have a price range, a *price bracket* or *price plateau*, in which they are prepared to buy.

You must price your product in that bracket, or justify its being outside of the bracket. The ball-barrow mentioned in chapter 3 has obvious advantages over the wheelbarrow, and these can be appreciated without having to use it. People have a good idea of the price of a wheelbarrow, so when the ball-barrow was on sale at a price outside of that price range the advantages could be seen to justify the higher price.

Your product might also have advantages over existing products, and this might be the very reason you have decided to go it alone. If the advantages can be readily understood and appreciated by customers, you can price above the normal range. If the advantages are not immediately observable, you may need extra publicity to get the message across about your improved product.

Influence of service

Service covers before-sales, during-sales and after-sales activities. The cost of service has to be recovered in the price. If your business involves the preparation of estimates, tenders and quotations, the cost of these must be in the price of the product.

Clearly you cannot quote for everything; you would spend all your time working for nothing. You must maintain a balance between, on the one hand, the number of quotations and tenders you prepare, and, on the other, your sales.

Similarly, if you deliver the product, install equipment, and provide training, guarantees, warranties and extend credit, the cost of all these must be contained in the price.

Many products require no after-sales service; but quite a number of convenience goods, toiletries, foodstuffs and everyday items require some before-sales service, such as window displays or testing facilities. This service has to be recovered in the price of the product. Service will be discussed in chapter 9.

Value-pricing strategy

Value-pricing strategy is also known as *skimming the market*. You set a high price for a small part of the market and it is creamed off. You maintain this price at a high level so that new customers have to upgrade themselves into the segment.

Following demand strategy

This is similar to value-pricing, but instead of keeping the price at a high level and persuading customers to upgrade themselves, it is scaled down at a controlled rate. The product often receives minor face-lifts and improvements to distinguish it from previous models. Sometimes its appearance, promotion, packaging and even its distribution method are changed to reflect the price reductions. The price is kept at each lower level long enough to mop up all available demand. As sales start to decline at a level, it's time to consider a price reduction.

Penetration pricing strategy

Penetration pricing, as the name indicates, consists of setting a very low price to enter and expand in a market as quickly as possible to secure cost advantages from volume production. This is not good strategy for the small business: the retaliation from competition can be too quick and too powerful.

Pre-emptive pricing strategy

A *pre-emptive pricing strategy* is similar to penetration pricing strategy, but used for a different purpose. It is to dissuade possible competitors from entering a market, or to achieve as many sales as possible before a competitor can enter. Price is set as near as possible to cost, with the result that profits are low and only attractive when sufficient volume is reached. A small business might use this strategy to concentrate on a small market segment, get in and out quickly and make a quick profit.

High-price and low-price policies

Each of these strategies may be described as a high-price or a low-price strategy. Consider a high-price policy if:

- Your product is unique, or is well-protected with patents.
- The product is difficult to develop or make.
- Price is not likely to be an important consideration for customers contemplating buying your product.
- The size of the market is likely to be too small to attract competition.
- A lot of effort is necessary to educate potential customers in the use of the product.
- You have limited financial resources and are unable – or do not wish to – raise extra money.

A low-price policy may be considered when conditions are the opposite of the above. It is not suggested that, if any of these conditions prevail, you must adopt a high-price or a low-price strategy; they merely emphasize that the particular policy has merit of being considered if some of the conditions exist.

For example, if you have limited finance, you should consider setting a high price, because a low price might not provide you with enough profit for expansion. However, a high price might attract early competition which, because of your limited resources, you would find difficult to counter. A thorough appraisal of the situation is needed to resolve the dilemma.

When they ask for a discount

A discount is a reduction from normal price. It serves a legitimate marketing purpose, but granting a discount is giving away part of your profit. Sooner or later you will be asked what discounts you are prepared to give, and unless you thoroughly understand the implictions of discounts, you are likely to pass up a lot of profit.

Quantity discount

Quantity discounts are given to induce buyers to purchase larger quantities, and vary according to the size of the order. Two types of quantity discount may be granted: cumulative and non-cumulative.

The *cumulative discount* encourages buyers to concentrate purchases of a product with one supplier. As the total of purchases increases during the year, the discount increases.

The more usual is *non-cumulative discount*; it applies to any one order and is determined by the size of the order. The purpose is to encourage buyers to place larger orders and enjoy a lower unit price. A small business should use this type of discount; the cumulative discount is for larger organizations who have the back-up facilities to record purchases.

Price list errors

Take care how you prepare your discount schedule; it can conceal traps. The price list in exhibit 4.6 has been extracted from an actual list circulated in February 1989 by a supplier of an office machine.

No. of machines	Unit price
1 to 9	£17
10 to 24	£15
25 and up	£14

Exhibit 4.6 Price list with discounts

The machine is priced at a basic £17. If ten to twenty-four units are bought, the price is £15; orders for twenty-five and up are at £14. This looks reasonable enough; an order for ten units would attract a discount of 12 per cent – £2 off £17. An order for twenty-five units attracts over 17 per cent – £3 off £17.

The actual situation is seen to be quite different when the price list is extended, as it has been in exhibit 4.7. For nine machines, a customer pays £153; ten machines cost £150 – *£3 less!* In effect this means that a customer who buys nine machines can have another one for free, *plus* £3. Also, twenty-five machines cost less than twenty-four. The price list has been prepared without looking at it from the viewpoint of the customer.

If you have a price list, extend it at the quantity/price change

No. of machines ordered	Unit price	Total
1	17	£17
9	17	£153
10	15	£150
24	15	£360
25	14	£350

Exhibit 4.7 Price list from exhibit 4.6 extended

points, and calculate what the customer has to pay for an extra one, or extra quantity, at the changed price.

Trade discount

A *trade discount* is given to middlemen who sell to stockists, or use the products to carry out services to others. Service middlemen, such as electricians, plumbers, hairdressers and builders use the products in their services to clients.

Wholesalers receive a trade discount because they buy in bulk, store, supply in smaller quantities, finance their customers, promote products and generally extend the distribution network for the manufacturer.

If you grant trade discounts, their type and size must follow industry practice. Packaged products distributed through wholesalers and retailers may carry a discount of 15 per cent for wholesalers and 25 per cent for retailers.

When quantity and trade discounts are given, the trade discount is deducted from the list price and the quantity discount applied to the new, reduced, base.

Cash discount

A *cash discount* is sometimes offered for early payment. A typical offer is 2 per cent within ten days, net thirty days; this is sometimes abbreviated on invoices to '2/10 net 30'. If the invoice is paid within ten days of the date of invoice, 2 per cent may be deducted from the net-of-tax total, or the full amount is paid thirty days from date of invoice.

The majority of sales are on a credit basis; even consumer purchasing is now normal with credit cards. Cash on delivery or cash in advance is rare except for those operations where, because there is no cost of financing credit, or of keeping credit records, the savings are passed on to the customer in the form of a lower price.

Your *terms* are the percentage reductions you are prepared to grant to customers who pay the invoice within a stated time period.

All your prices and price schedules should include a percentage oncost to cover the normal credit you grant. Usually this is one month after receipt of statement. Effectively this can provide nearly two months credit to customers.

It's your money!

Immediately you have made a sale and delivered the product or supplied the service, what the customer owes you is *your money*. If the purchase has been made on credit, the moment that payment changes from being due to being overdue, that money is a free loan by you to the customer.

If customers delay payment, and use your money in this way, you have to increase your working capital to fund them. If you are borrowing money from the bank, it means, in effect, that you are borrowing your own money and paying the bank interest for the privilege!

Being lax with your settlement terms or the way you collect moneys due to you is the same as cutting your prices. If you are getting sales because you allow customers liberal credit, your price must include a good margin for this.

How to control credit

If you intend to sell on credit terms, categorize your customers to represent their credit-worthiness and punctuality in paying. You could colour-code them – say, blue, green, red:

- *Blue* customers pay their invoices on time according to the terms on the invoice.
- *Green* customers are slow payers and do not comply with the terms on the invoice. They will use your money as long as you let them.
- *Red* customers are cash with order or on a proforma invoice basis because they represent too much of a risk.

Invoices and statements

Have simple invoices that are easy to understand, with subtotals, discounts and VAT clearly marked, leading to the total sum to be paid.

Make it easy for your customers to pay your invoices. Have a rubber stamp prepared to stamp them, so that you can insert how much may be deducted if it is paid within the stated period.

Prepare and send statements regularly, with four sections, or at least four clearly understandable summaries: payments received, invoices submitted but not due for payment, invoices and their total due for payment, invoices overdue.

Payments due

Have a list – a computer printout if possible – of payments due each day, or at least each week, depending on the volume of work and money involved. Include on this list all amounts overdue and how long they are overdue.

Overdue payments

Issue overdue statements to customers. Remind slow-paying customers four days or so after payment is due if the amount is still outstanding. Issue an overdue statement listing the invoices not paid and endorse with words such as, 'This statement contains items that are now overdue. Please phone 01-234 5678 if there is any reason why payment is being withheld.'

If you get no response or payment after an overdue statement has been issued, telephone the customer and establish contact with someone with appropriate authority. Obtain agreement that there are no queries on the invoices and put the substance of the telephone conversation in writing to the person concerned.

If items are in dispute, send an amended statement listing the amounts not in dispute but overdue for payment, and show the disputed items separately.

Key points

- A high price gives a high profit but makes a product more difficult to sell.
- If you use cost-pricing, develop a standard mark-up procedure to make your pricing easy.
- Always extend your price list at the quantity change points to check for errors.
- When you give a discount, you are giving away some of your profit.
- From the start, have a system that gets *your money* in when it is due.

5

Distribution

Outline

Distribution is getting the right products to the right people when they need them. We look at:

- channels for consumer products
- channels for industrial products
- methods used in the channels
- the advantages of franchising
- intensive, selective and exclusive distribution
- the total market, or a part of it?
- the best marketing strategy for the small business

Getting your product or service to users

If you are making a product, it will earn you no money while it stays in your back room, garage, store, factory or warehouse; if it is a service you are offering, until someone makes use of it, it will be a dead loss.

All the time a product just sits there, doing nothing, it is costing you money. There is the cost of raw materials and components used in its manufacture, the labour to make it, the overheads and servicing costs, and it is taking up storage space which you may have to pay for. Products must be distributed; services must be rendered.

Two main ways to distribute

Whatever business you have decided to start, there are two main ways you can get your product or service into the hands of the user:

you can sell it directly to the user or you can sell it through a middleman.

Distributing through a middleman relieves you of a lot of the tedium of finding customers and then having to sell to them. Normally you can only sell to one user at a time, so each time you try to make a sale you have to go through your sales presentation. One thing is for sure: with such practice, you will certainly become skilled at telling the tale!

Selling to a middleman usually means that you sell more than one at a time; it's like killing several birds with one stone.

There are often two middlemen between you and the user: in the consumer market there are wholesalers and retailers. Wholesalers buy in gross lots; the retailer in dozens. Trying to sell to either doesn't make a lot of sense if you can only produce one a day!

With industrial products, although many sales are made direct to users, distribution is often through authorized stockists or official agents.

If your production is limited, analyse the situation carefully before going to middlemen. You might stimulate a level of interest and demand that you couldn't satisfy, and simply open the way for a competitor.

In contrast, if you can produce large quantities of your products, selling to middlemen might be the easiest way of distributing them.

If you sell direct to the user, you pocket all the profits but you have to be efficient. You would have to distribute the products as effectively as the professional distributors and at a similar cost. Distributors have often invested considerable sums in warehousing and transportation over the years, and while you could be as efficient as the current distributors the necessary investment to compete effectively might be astronomical.

Your production capability and financial resources are the first influences on your choice of distribution channel. The next influence is the way that competitors distribute their products in the particular market. The methods they use have been tested and proved, and although you would be unwise to ignore current practice, you can often gain advantages by adopting a different distribution method while maintaining a degree of flexibility. Many companies have a policy of distributing their products through wholesalers under one brand name, and, differently packaged, through appointed retailers under another. Obviously you need a lot of production capacity to distribute through different channels.

Distribution of consumer products

If you have a consumer product or service, you will need to keep abreast of the changing distribution pattern for consumer products, so that you can develop your operations where you have the best chance of success.

There are three main channels: direct to users, through retailers and through wholesalers. A fourth has also developed in recent years: through wholesalers as cash-and-carry operators, or discount houses, to users. The distribution pattern is illustrated in exhibit 5.1.

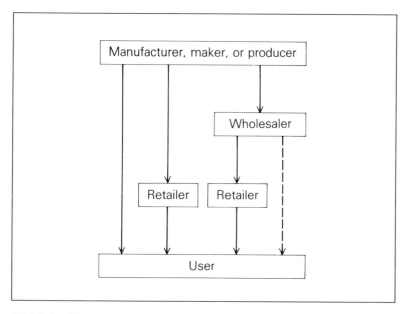

Exhibit 5.1 Three consumer distribution channels

Before 1960 about 60 per cent of consumer goods were distributed through wholesale channels, and 30 per cent through retailers. From the 1960s to the late 1980s the pattern changed; retail outlets expanded their operations at the expense of wholesalers. Now over 70 per cent of all consumer trade flows through retail outlets, and under 20 per cent through wholesalers; about 5 per cent is direct to the user from the manufacturer. In the food and drink trade, where wholesalers used to be dominant, they now distribute only 15 per cent; 85 per cent is through retail organizations.

The reason why manufacturers moved closer to retailers and supplied direct was to increase their control over marketing to consumers. At the same time, retailers began to combine in groups with considerable purchasing power and buy direct from manufacturers. The grocery trade has led the way in changing distribution patterns. The large grocery retailing groups such as Safeway, Gateway, Sainsbury and Tesco now have nearly 2,000 large stores throughout the UK – about 25 per cent of them are superstores.

This squeezing of wholesalers from both sides stimulated them into retaliatory actions. First they created co-operative groups. A wholesaler and a number of retailers would form a voluntary group, the retailers being required to place a minimum percentage of their orders with the wholesaler. The grocery trade was the first to see such groups, where they operate under a common symbol such as Londis, Mace, Spar and VG, and benefit from group advertising and – because of their total purchasing power – low prices.

Voluntary groups have developed in many other trades. The largest is in the pharmaceutical trade, with over 10,000 members. Others are confectionery, tobacco and newsagents (CTN), with between 6,000 and 7,000 members; florists, with nearly 3,000; home decoration; health foods; photographic supplies; computers; car accessories; garages; sports goods; toys.

Wholesalers then started aggressive retail selling activities – cash-and-carry and discount houses. It is not unusual to find a wholesaler with a cash-and-carry operation at one end of the premises and a traditional wholesaling operation at the other.

The second half of the 1980s saw the development of *convenience* stores. These are large self-service stores which specialize in one main trade, are open seven days a week for long hours, and have adequate car parking space. The areas they operate in are groceries, do-it-yourself, the CTN trade, and car accessories.

Clearly, the distinguishing lines between retailers and wholesalers have been largely eroded. The 'Trade Only' signs that used to be seen in wholesale outlets have mostly disappeared.

Franchise operations

Commercial franchising, which developed in the USA, is a fast-developing distribution channel in the UK and continental Europe. The voluntary groups mentioned above are a form of franchise. In the UK there are approximately 500 different franchise operations and over 25,000 franchised businesses. There are three different marketing systems:

- manufacture under licence of a proprietary product (e.g. soft drinks, mattresses, clothes and the right to apply the licensor's trademark to the products);
- distributor agreements (e.g. motor cars, petrol and fuel);
- contractual licence under which the franchisee operates a business under the trade name of the franchisor.

It is the third type of franchising that is most applicable to the small business. Some of the franchises – car engine tuning, car valeting, carpet cleaning, damp-proofing, domestic cleaning, drain and pipe cleaning, milk rounds, office cleaning, repair services, timber treatment – can be organized and run from home because they are mainly servicing operations. The majority of franchises require considerable investment by the franchisee for premises, shops, transport, equipment and, for Holiday Inns, a hotel!

Nevertheless, there are several opportunities for the enthusiastic and energetic small business person who is willing to conduct business as dictated by the franchisor, in return for continuing publicity, advice and assistance.

The franchisor should normally conduct market research, but, if you intend to set up in your own locality, you should carry out your own market investigation because you know the area better than the franchisor. The problems of the catchment area were discussed in chapter 2. In franchising, this area is of crucial importance; if you are going to take up a franchise, make sure you investigate the potential area.

Industrial distribution

Industrial products are distributed mainly through two channels: direct to the user of the product or through one intermediary, typically a stockist or the manufacturer's appointed sales agent.

The type of distribution used by a manufacturer will affect the price structure. Prices and discounts accorded to each type of middleman are related to the amount of service to be provided to those lower in the distribution network. In hi-tech fields such as computer software, prices reflect the amount of customer support necessary: training, development and upgrading. Typically such a distribution network consists of distributors, value-added remarketers and users.

Of the four main types of industrial products discussed in chapter 3, capital equipment, substantial materials, supplies and major consultancy services are normally sold direct from supplier to industry, with no middlemen being involved. In addition, the acquisition of capital equipment and major items of expenditure have to be sanctioned by the board of directors. The purchase of bulk materials and supplies is usually negotiated by buyers with suppliers, and deliveries arranged in line with the needs of production.

Minor items such as small tools, screws, cleaning materials, office sundries, paper and photography are supplied by a distributor or small businesses.

Distribution methods

Different methods can be used in the channels of distribution. Consider first some methods of distribution direct from the maker to the user.

A commonly used method is mail order. Adverts are placed in appropriate media inviting readers to purchase directly from the maker.

Another method that is often adopted by the small business is to load products into a van and sell them round the streets, at a market, or even in a field at a boot sale. The founder of a well-known personal computer company started in this way, selling television aerials from the roof-rack of his car at open markets.

A third example is door-to-door selling. This can be tightly controlled, concentrating on one area at a time, and can either be conducted by the owner of the business alone or with a team of sales people.

In a fourth method the producer has a sales point where the product is made or grown, and sells direct to people who call. This method is typical of garden centres, and is often adopted for farm produce. Adjacent to the growing area the grower has a stall or shed from which sales are made. The method is also found in some consumer product factories which have a sales office. Where the manufacturer might offend retailers in the locality, a policy of selling 'seconds' is adopted. Sometimes even the most rigorous inspection of the merchandise fails to identify the reason why it has been downgraded to a second quality product!

And a fifth example: to maintain complete control over sales and marketing, producers acquire their own retail outlets from which to sell their products. This method has been adopted by some of the large shoe manufacturers.

That makes five different methods of selling in one channel. In each of the other channels some of these methods could be used. Your choice of channel is likely to be direct to the user; before you decide on the method, you must define your target market. Is it possible for you to tackle all possible buying points? If not, how do you make a selection?

Selecting the distribution channel

When you are considering which method of distribution to use, the first two influences mentioned earlier in this chapter – production capability and financial resources – are the overriding constraints.

If your production capacity is limited, there is no way that you can undertake national distribution: select a small geographical area, a limited number of users, or a middleman who is able to take your output.

Your choice must be within your financial capability. You may prefer to distribute to a limited number of users, but if these are widely spread around the country, you may not be able to service them with your available finance and physical resources.

If these considerations lead you to think of restricting your distribution to a limited area, make sure it contains sufficient potential customers.

Three degrees of distribution

When selling through a trade channel, irrespective of the method chosen, there are three main degrees of distribution: intensive, selective and exclusive.

Intensive distribution means that you sell to every possible outlet in the chosen market. If they'll stock it, you'll sell it to them. This means that you don't pick and choose; you don't prejudge any outlet because you think it's in the wrong place, or has the wrong image, or you don't like the look of it. Intensive distribution means selling to everyone who is willing to purchase.

Selective distribution is restricting sales to one outlet for every area or district. As turnover increases in an area another outlet is selected. The aim is to seek an optimum number of outlets that will give adequate market coverage, but not so many that you have to deal with a large number of outlets, each with a small total purchase.

Exclusive distribution is giving one outlet the sole right to sell a product in any one area. The agreement between the supplier and the outlet specifies the area of influence, the minimum turnover expected and the period of the agreement. All enquiries from the area are passed to the exclusive stockist. Such a degree of distribution can give the product an enhanced image. This often means it carries a higher profit margin, which is intended to encourage the dealer to sell the product more aggressively.

Unless you have set up business as a distributor or sole agent for a manufacturer on an exclusive basis, you should adopt intensive distribution for your product or service.

Selecting the distribution method

Three main methods are commonly used by the small business to sell direct to the user:

- sales calls on buyers in factories, or people at home;
- 'party plan' sales by commission-only agents (typically, an agent arranges a coffee morning and invites a number of people to view the merchandise);
- mail order, using press advertising, letters or catalogues to get the information out, and the postal system or carrier service to deliver the goods. Although called 'mail' order, the postal system is often not used at all: advertisements are placed in appropriate media, orders are received by telephone and the goods are delivered by carrier.

If you distribute through one middleman, you will be selling to retail outlets or industrial stockists.

Independent shops form the largest number of retail outlets – 200,000 of nearly 350,000 in the UK. But, while nearly 60 per cent are independent retailers, they achieve only 30 per cent of the total retail trade. There are about 71,000 multiple retailers, 65,000 super-markets and nearly 6,000 co-operative societies.

Whichever type of retail outlet you choose, the task on a national basis is formidable, and may be beyond the capability of a small business. You would need to refine retailers into smaller groups, using the Yellow Pages of telephone directories.

These directories also have classified lists for specific products and industrial companies. While deciding which types of retailers you intend to approach is fairly straightforward, deciding which industrial organizations to approach requires further analysis.

For potential industrial customers it is better to use one of the trade directories in your local reference library. If you are going to approach manufacturers of specific products and equipment, you'll find suitable lists in the appropriate directory. Most of them contain essential data on companies that will enable you to refine your survey to your needs. By an intelligent interpretation of the data you can gauge the size and potential of the organization. Companies with several divisional and functional directors (such as finance, engineering, research, purchasing, marketing and personnel) are likely to be substantial outfits.

You can approach your prospective customers with letters, phone calls or personal visits. In view of the size of the task, a combination of telephone call and personal visit is the best method for the small business.

Having made your initial choice, you then consider competitive activities in the selected channel. Will the method you propose to use be similar to competitors' operations, or different from them? Will it give you an advantage, or put you at a disadvantage?

Choose the distribution method that gives you the greatest control and flexibility. You must be able to control the marketing operation: geographical distribution, rate of penetration of the market, promotion and sales.

Your techniques must be flexible to permit changes when necessary or desirable. If you start activities that you cannot subsequently control, you will have created a market for a competitor with larger resources. You must balance what is possible from your production capacity with what the selected target market will absorb.

Market coverage and penetration

You will often hear of market coverage, market penetration and, sometimes, market reach. Market surveys often include the term market saturation.

Market coverage is the extent to which a supplier can reach potential customers in an area. If a company has 95 per cent market coverage, it means that customers in 95 per cent of the total market are able to obtain the product or service of the company.

Market penetration is the degree to which a company has established active connections in a distribution channel; customers are actively buying the product or service, and have been doing so for some time. A weaker definition of penetration is market share: the percentage share of the total market. But, as you saw in chapter 1, market share can be defined in different ways: as a percentage of total volume sales, value sales, trade or industry sales, sector sales, percentage of outlets etc.

Market reach is sometimes used to indicate coverage, and sometimes to indicate penetration.

Market saturation is often linked with market penetration in market research. In a survey of domestic electric clocks, penetration could mean the percentage of households having at least one electric clock, and saturation the percentage of households having more than one. But be careful: in continental Europe the meaning of the two terms is often reversed.

Should you have need to interpret a market research report, always obtain a definition of the terms used.

Target market

Let us assume that you have obtained data on the total market for your product, and that your potential customers are spread throughout the country as illustrated diagrammatically in exhibit 5.2. This is not necessarily a geographical spread, but an abstract, or conceptual, spread.

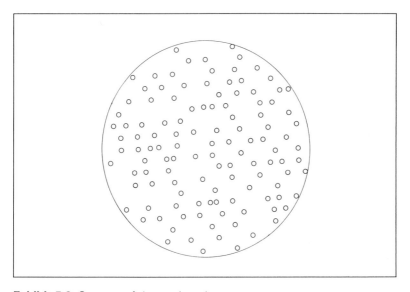

Exhibit 5.2 Concept of the total market

Suppose you had formulated a new non-alcoholic beer. The product would have universal appeal, so the total market would be every possible outlet that could purchase your product, as shown in exhibit 5.2. This could represent a geographical spread of outlets, or simply the total number of outlets all jumbled together: cafés, supermarkets, stores, shops, public houses, hotels, restaurants, garages etc. – in fact, anywhere where it would be possible to sell the product.

This total market could be divided into sub-markets: the licensed trade, restaurants, cafés, supermarkets, small independent shops, garage forecourts, cinemas, showgrounds, mobile shops and so on. This segmented market is illustrated diagrammatically in exhibit 5.3.

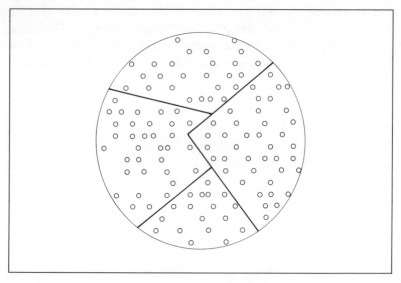

Exhibit 5.3 Segmented market

Undifferentiated, differentiated and concentrated marketing

You can market your product to the total market or to segments of it. There are three ways of doing this. Each has a long name, but each has a simple explanation of its strategy; they are undifferentiated marketing, differentiated marketing and concentrated marketing.

Undifferentiated marketing means that you do not distinguish between types of outlet or different segments; you market one type of product. It doesn't matter to whom you sell – user, corner shop, supermarket, wholesaler, small factory, or multinational organization – you have one product, one name, one price structure, and one advertising and promotional theme.

Differentiated marketing means selling a different version of the product or a different pack to different segments. You identify segments of the total market that have similar characteristics, and market a product that has been specially designed or packaged for that segment.

Wholesalers, retailers, departmental stores, licensed trade, hotels, small metal-working shops, electrical engineering factories, wood mills, laundries, dry-cleaning establishments – whatever the type of outlet, you combine them into suitable market segments. The product, packaging, its name and price structure is appropriate for that segment. Your advertising and promotion messages are designed for specific segments, focusing on the needs of its members and the uses they require of the product.

Whereas undifferentiated and differentiated marketing imply that the total market is tackled, *concentrated marketing* is restricting operations to a segment of the market. One segment is selected and concentrated on to the exclusion of the rest of the market. The type or model of product, its price, advertising and promotion, distribution channel and method of selling are developed for that segment.

Which marketing strategy?

The very fact that you are starting a small business means that your production and finance resources are limited in the beginning. Of the three marketing strategies mentioned above, the most costly is going for the total market and differentiating the approach to each segment. The method that requires least funding is concentrated marketing. So that is the strategy you should adopt, directing your efforts to a chosen segment. The amount of selling and marketing fire-power you can focus on a small part of the market can equal, or even be greater than, some of your competitors. In addition you have the advantages of flexibility.

As your business develops, your expansion should be segment by segment, choosing each with care to avoid having to make too many costly adaptations early in your business life. The profits you generate are used to finance your expansion.

Market segmentation

Whatever marketing strategy you adopt, be absolutely clear that a single market does not, and cannot, exist, no matter what directions emanate from Brussels, Strasbourg or Luxembourg. In marketing terms, a single market is only possible if you are selling to robots.

Human beings are complex individuals, and they are even more complicated when in groups. Living conditions, social mores and working practices vary throughout the country; the variations are greater between different countries. If you only take average weather into consideration, you can appreciate that different geographical locations have different characteristics, and people living there have different needs.

Varying degrees of water hardness require different formulations of soap and detergent. Travel to France, Belgium and Germany and you will realize that the idea of a single market for electrical plugs and sockets might exist in the future but certainly not in 1992.

People who think that all will be changed come 1 January 1993 are living in a parochial marketing cloud: they certainly demonstrate no understanding of marketing realities.

As a small business person you cannot afford to make the mistake of assuming that all parts of the market are the same. Your future success lies in your ability to distinguish between one segment and another, and to concentrate your marketing activities on making profits from the segments you choose.

To segment a market adequately it must be:

- accessible;
- measurable;
- substantial;
- different enough to be distinguishable;
- durable.

'Accessible' means that you can get at it. You can advertise to potential customers in the segment without wasting too much money advertising to others. If the people or companies who make up the segment are scattered throughout the country, belong to no association, or have no common communication channel, they are not accessible as a segment.

It is possible to segment a total market using criteria such as people's income levels. These groups exist, but you can't get at them: there is no way you can advertise to them or go into the market and sell to them. To sell to a segment, it must be accessible.

A segment must be measurable. If it's not possible to determine how many potential customers it has, the segment may be fictitious, or the numbers insignificant. A segment that cannot be measured is an enigma: you don't know what sales and marketing resources to devote to it, because you don't know how big it is.

A market segment must be substantial. It's no use defining a segment and then finding that it contains only a few customers. Your pricing strategy could influence the size of the segment: reduce your price by a half, and you might increase its size considerably. However, as price tends to be related to quality in customers' minds, reducing your price could just as easily reduce the size of the segment.

A market segment must be sufficiently different from other parts of the market for products and prices to appeal only to that segment. If you cannot restrict your advertising, distribution and selling efforts to the segment, there is little point in segmenting the market. Prices offered to a segment thought to be unique may be taken up by the market generally. If the market segment cannot be distinguished, you cannot make sufficiently different appeals to it.

A market segment should be durable, not volatile. If your business is to be built by concentrating on particular segments, they should be there next year and the year after. If they are not, a lot of goodwill and investment in marketing activities will be wasted.

Segment characteristics

Some of the characteristics that you can use to segment a market for a product or service are:

- geographic location;
- age or sex;

- the standard, type and location of house;
- the size of organization requiring service;
- specific product or service requirements;
- SIC industry group;
- benefits derived from product or service.

Distribution costs

Find out the average distribution costs, especially transport and warehousing, for the industry in which you are operating. Your costs should be comparable with these, and if you are to develop a really profitable business, they should be below average costs.

Not all of the following will be applicable to your business at the start, but it is good policy to have a broad distribution plan for the future, and relate all your decisions, especially the early ones, to that plan. Depending on the nature of your business and the frequency that changes take place, determine current costs from time to time of:

- warehousing space;
- packaging materials;
- heat, light and power;
- salaries and wages of all engaged in distribution;
- drivers' and mileage allowances;
- local, national and international carrier costs;
- postage.

You may think that establishing some of these costs, such as warehouse space, may be a fruitless exercise if you are storing your products in your spare room or garage. Nevertheless, they must be realistically estimated so that when you expand and have to use – and pay for – separate storage space, adequate costs are already included in your price structure. Analyse the main distribution costs as percentages of sales and also of all overheads. This will be looked at in more detail in chapter 10.

As you expand your business and increase sales, you increase your distribution operations. You must determine the amount of growth you can cope with before needing any of the following which may apply to your business:

- extra storage space;
- modified layout;
- additional handling equipment;
- additional labour;
- improved loading facilities;
- revised stock control procedures;
- revised documentation;
- appointment of supervision;
- security measures;
- computerized distribution.

A shoe product

Suppose that you had a product of interest to shoe shops. There are about 12,000 of these in the UK: it would be a daunting task to approach this number of outlets. Further investigations reveal that half of them belong to about ten multiple retail groups that operate thirty different retail chains. If each shoe chain buys centrally for its group of shops, that is about thirty buying points for these multiple retailers. Persuade these thirty buying offices of the worth of your product, and you are on the way to having it distributed to about 6,000 retail outlets.

Thus the best distribution strategy is to concentrate on one segment and sell to stockists.

You would need to call on a cross-section of shoe shops and departments in departmental stores in the area, find out how they buy, and establish the name of the buyer and location. Arrange a meeting with, say, six to ten buyers, and from the first meeting develop your presentation. As you see more buyers you will gain more market information, and will be able to focus your discussions more accurately. Offer to supply your product from stock and guarantee a delivery period.

A speciality for the licensed trade

In 1987 a newly-started sales agent in Swindon obtained the sole UK selling rights of a small, low-priced, over-the-counter item of interest to public house customers. The product does not conflict with any contract between the licensee and the brewery. Free houses, those not tied to any particular brewery, may purchase anywhere. It is suitably packaged and can be sold on a cash basis.

There are approximately 140,000 licensed premises in the UK. A handful of large brewery groups own about 35,000 public houses, 4,000 off-licenses and nearly 300 hotels. The number of free houses is between 25,000 and 30,000.

Having given the agent the sole UK selling rights, the principal naturally expects substantial sales. Therefore it is not a situation where the agent can personally carry out all the selling.

The best distribution policy is a concentrated strategy, and the agent did just this. He first tested a market segment, getting information from Yellow Pages, and called on every public house in an area. With this first-hand knowledge he developed a sales presentation, then advertised for, and appointed, agents throughout the country.

He stipulated that they must already be carrying lines to public houses, and that his product was to be considered as a profitable sideline. As he wanted to attract good agents, the quality of his advertisements, letter heading and all sales literature were of a high standard. He asked for details of what the agents were currently carrying so that he could better judge their worth. To project confidence he gave names of his bankers and solicitor.

As you might expect, his main problem has always been to find good agents. The appointed agent pays for the display card of samples, and has to achieve an agreed sales turnover after three months. A small payment and a modest sales objective, but it sorts out the men from the boys.

As at the end of May 1989 his sales are high, having increased every month since he started, and the principal has already invited him to take on more lines. From being a sole agent, for one product, he is now about to embark on the profitable career of a manufacturer's agent.

An electronic hand-dryer

In the early 1980s a tiny company based in Derbyshire started marketing a hand-dryer assembled from bought-in components.

The dryer is activated automatically when the hands are inserted, and switches off three seconds after they are removed from the stream of warm air. Customers include all commercial and industrial establishments where there are facilities for washing hands.

The company was advised to distribute direct to user, using personal selling, and start with a concentrated marketing strategy; to tackle the whole market was well beyond its resources.

The owner of the business carried out the initial selling and distribution to establish the best method of making a presentation. Operations were extended, segment by segment, in line with increasing production. Sales agents were appointed for nominated territories; each was required to buy the sample dryer and achieve a minimum turnover in six months.

If you are contemplating operating a similar business, remember that when you appoint agents on a commission-only basis, you should supply them with a sample product on payment of its cost price. Do not appoint agents and supply them with free samples: it is the quickest way to get rid of your stock. By requiring agents to pay for the product, only those who have serious intentions of selling will be interested. However, finding good agents is very difficult, and most of your time will be devoted to searching for them; those you do appoint should prove to be first-class sales people.

Some distribution dos and don'ts

- Regularly update your market intelligence on the total number of potential outlets in a segment.
- Classify outlets by size and potential, and update the classification annually.
- Review your distribution policy at least every year.
- Ensure that customers are not often out of stock.
- Maintenance of customer stock levels should be comparable with competitive servicing.
- Periodically survey customers to establish their satisfaction with services appropriate to the product: delivery, installation, spares, repairs, back-up, accounts etc.

● If you sell a repeat-purchase product, don't expand your business at the expense of present customers who provide you with profit; devote 80 per cent of your time and energies to them.

Key points

● Expose your product as widely as possible.
● For the small business, direct-to-user is the best policy to adopt at first.
● In your early days you probably can't afford to be selective or exclusive; distribute intensively.
● In marketing terms there is no such thing as a single market.
● Keep a tight control on all distribution costs.

6

Advertising

Advertising: choices and pitfalls

In the total marketing context, promotion covers everything that spreads the word about a product with the aim of selling it. It includes all advertising, publicity, sales promotion, sales literature, press relations and personal selling. In this chapter we concentrate on advertising; promotion and selling are examined in chapters 7 and 8.

Every day we are bombarded with adverts on television, on posters, in newspapers and in magazines for products we shall never buy. That advertising is a waste of the advertisers' money as far as we are concerned. Some advertising goes to the wrong people, for the wrong product, at the wrong price and at the wrong time. A part of advertising is also wasted because, although it's 'seen', it doesn't register with the viewer or reader. A general aim of this chapter is to help you keep such wastage to a minimum.

Where do you start? How do you promote the product? How do you advertise? Is it worth advertising in the local paper? What about a professional journal? Trade or industrial magazines? The national dailies? Television? Radio? There is no shortage of choice, so we start by focusing on your potential customers.

Targeting your customers

Relate your product, and the way you advertise and sell it, to a specific target market. This is product/market planning, whether for selling or publicity. Decide who will be your customers. They could be individual men or women, people in a particular age group, people in a certain social group or other special group, children up to the age of 14, children who live in towns, buyers in shops, departmental store buyers, buyers in manufacturers. Or the customers could be even more closely defined, such as buyers in companies in a certain area who make a given product. Write a description of the people you consider are your targets, using the following as models:

- buyers for companies fabricating sheet metal constructions, using mechanical and electrical equipment, and situated within 40 miles of Coventry;
- couples with children in houses with gardens, living on private housing estates in High Wycombe;
- manufacturers of 'instant hot water' shower units in the UK, France, West Germany and Denmark.

Promoting your product

Once it is known that you have a product or service to market, you will receive a lot of advice on the best way to advertise it, and many invitations to advertise in the 'best' media.

Spending money on advertising is easy: spending it to get your message across to generate enquiries and sales is difficult.

Before you spend anything on promotion, use word-of-mouth. Tell people what you have for sale. In fact, tell everyone: tell your family, your friends, previous colleagues, people you see socially, or at meetings and functions. Everyone you meet should know what you have for sale. Tell them about your product, and be prepared to sell it at any time. Always carry visiting cards and, if appropriate, sales literature and a price list.

This early enthusiasm will help you in two ways: the sales you make will give you confidence to develop your business; people's questions and responses to your explanations will indicate how you should advertise your product.

How you propose to distribute your product will influence how you promote it. If you deal directly with users, you advertise to users; if you market through intermediaries, you promote to both intermediaries and users.

Unique selling points

You still hear people talking of *unique selling points* or USPs. They tell you to look for the USPs in your product and emphasize them in your advertising, your literature, your sales presentations.

If marketing is considering business from the viewpoint of the customer, it's not USPs we should be looking for, but UBPs – unique buying points – the reasons why potential customers should *buy* your product in preference to another.

The main reason why some products fail is that customers do not want them or see no tangible benefits in them. It doesn't matter how many USPs they possess, they don't have any UBPs!

Promoting the USPs of your product is promoting its attributes; you have to concentrate on its benefits – benefits to the customer who will use it.

Before drawing up plans and promotional strategies, put down on paper a list of the attributes of the product or service you intend to supply, and at the side of each, a customer benefit. Not every attribute will have a direct benefit. You must put your thinking cap on and work out benefits that can flow from the attributes: what advantage, gain, profit, value, or good will the user receive from the use of the product. Often you can devise several benefits from one

Attribute	Benefit
Weighs 2 kg	*Heavy*
	Solid, heavy construction
	Adequate weight for the job
	Won't blow away
	Light
	Light, easy to use
	Effortless in operation
	Readily portable
	A child could carry it
Measures 6 cm × 4 cm	*Small*
	Fits neatly in the hand
	Ideal for the purse
	Unobtrusive but powerful
	Large
	Won't be lost in your tool box
	Easily seen
	Sensible size for easy use
Possesses university degree in horticulture	Complete garden design
	Most suitable plants
	Plant for year-round beauty
	Easy-gardening planning
	Regular expert maintenance

Exhibit 6.1 Attributes and benefits

attribute. Exhibit 6.1 provides some simple, general examples to indicate how attributes can be benefits in different, sometimes opposite, directions depending on the product.

Local publicity

Let us assume that you are starting a gardening service. Your market is to be within a few miles of your home, and you will concentrate on houses with large gardens, offering your service direct. You decide to advertise.

Start with the most simple of advertising media – postcard advertising. Survey the locality and see which shops display advertising cards. If there are large offices, factories and other establishments in the area, call and see if it is possible to have a postcard displayed on the staff notice-board, canteen, or other convenient place. If you are unable to make contact with the person who can authorize it, write to the company with your proposition, enclosing a copy of the post-card advert.

Don't prejudge any possible site; don't decide that you won't advertise in a particular shop because you don't like the look of it, it's in the wrong area, or for some other reason. It never ceases to surprise the author what works in advertising and marketing (or for that matter, in books).

During your survey of possible sites, you will learn whether it is a feasible operation or not. As soon as you have locations for your cards, prepare them. Don't rush this in a few minutes over breakfast; devote time and thought to the exercise. Draft your message and test it on family and friends. Don't prejudge the wording: you never know what brings results. If you have two or three ideas, try them all, using different locations. Try to put the message over succinctly, like 'Fire!' to clear a building quickly. Alternative suggestions are given in exhibits 6.2 and 6.3.

GARDENING SERVICE

Qualified, young, energetic, horticulturist, with several years' training and experience, available to help you construct and maintain your garden, irrespective of its size. Skilled garden layouts, and able to undertake weekly maintenance. Possess all necessary equipment; reasonable rates.

Phone John Gardner 01–234 5678.

Exhibit 6.2 First postcard advert

The first is a straightforward announcement, selling attributes. The heading is likely to be seen by most people who look at the cards. Those who have no interest in gardening won't read beyond the headline; people who do may read further. The words 'available

---

GARDENING

Eliminate gardening backache. I'll do the work; you enjoy the garden. Costs won't hurt your wallet! Phone me, evenings if possible, 01–234 5678.

John Gardner
BSc (Horticulture)

Exhibit 6.3 Second postcard advert

to help you' will attract potential customers to read on. But the latter part of the message is still selling attributes: it's 'selling the steak, not the sizzle'.

The second has a number of positive points. When we scan a piece of writing or print quickly, we don't read every word from left to right, and often the eye runs down the page. If your name was somewhere on the page, you would tend to spot it immediately: 'It jumps out of the page'. It's the same with emotive words such as 'money', 'sex', 'murder', 'free' and so on. These facts give the second postcard considerable merit. It is short, amusing, can be read quickly, and combines the selling of benefits with a statement about the expertise of the advertiser.

The headline and first few words, especially the position of the headline above the word 'backache', will register with many people and persuade them to read on. People who just glance at the ad will probably notice the words 'garden' and 'backache'. This second card is likely to stimulate potential customers into finding out 'How much?'

While this analysis is justifiable, you can never judge publicity before it is tried. You cannot say, 'This *is* a good advertisement'; only, 'That *was* a good advertisement.' It has to be judged in retrospect.

Classified advertisements

There are two main types of newspaper and magazine advertising – *display* and *classified*. Classified ads are bought on the basis of number of words or by the line – usually with a minimum number of lines. Some papers have *semi-display* ads which are set in the classified section with a border.

Classifieds are comparatively inexpensive and normally have a high readership. You can tell whether a particular publication is a popular medium for classified advertising by inspecting a few back issues. They are grouped in sections of interest: motoring, gardening, do-it-yourself, personal etc., and usually in alphabetical order.

To get your classified announcement noticed, use words that offer benefits and have emotive appeal. The following six words have had a lot of advertising money spent on them: 'cool', 'new', 'power', 'relief', 'refreshing', 'white'. Keep your message to the telegraphic minimum. The shortest and most succinct letter ever written is supposed to be from a man to his landlord who had asked him to vacate an apartment. He replied, 'I remain, yours sincerely.'

Classifieds can be flexible, with insertions in consecutive editions, or more than one in the same issue. Change the wording from time to time to keep the announcement fresh and dynamic, but repeat the basic message. Even when you have sufficient business from your efforts, you should not stop advertising entirely. The occasional advert maintains your contact with the market, and you never know when you are going to lose business for reasons beyond your control.

Local newspapers

The UK is not short of newspapers; every district has its local rag. Circulation is related to the population of the area they cover. Large counties have a series of local editions, often under different local names. Some of these are distributed free, the cost of their production being paid for by the advertising. A few offer free adverts, limited to two or three lines. The first postcard could be condensed:

Qualified, experienced, horticulturist available to help you with your garden. Possess all necessary equipment and transport. Phone 01–234 5678

A version of the second might be more appealing:

Eliminate garden backache. I'll do the work, you enjoy the garden. Evenings: John Gardner 01–234 5678

Direct mail

Don't confuse direct mail with mail order. Mail order is a distribution method; direct mail is a form of publicity. It is 'direct' because it is aimed at the person you want to receive it; 'mail' because the postal system is used.

You probably get your share of direct mail, and are given the opportunity of winning yet another £30,000, a motor car, or whatever the advertiser is offering as an inducement for your custom. Often you are told that you have been specially selected to participate in some draw or contest. All of these highly personalized mailings are the output of the computer and laser printer. A high proportion of such mailings is filed straight into the waste-paper basket.

At least 2,000 million items, costing around £500m, are classified by the Post Office as direct mail. It is an effective, reasonable cost method of getting your message to the right people. As with all advertising, *the medium is more important than the message*. No matter how powerful the message, if it doesn't reach the right person, it's wasted. Your task is to get a simple, factual message *to the right person*.

Direct mail objectives

Before you start direct mail activities, decide what it is you want to achieve. You may wish to notify people of your change of address, sell a product, sell a service, have people phone you, try to get appointments, get people to visit you, or simply to publicize what you are doing.

An objective should be written in terms of the results you desire to be achieved. If you wish to obtain appointments with people, decide on a number that will satisfy you. Say you are mailing 200 people. Your objective could be to get appointments with 15 per cent of them – thirty people.

If you are selling a service and mailing thirty householders, you could set your objective at, say, six to accept your offer. By committing your objective to writing, you focus your efforts on what you are trying to achieve.

Direct mail lists

The most important element in direct mail advertising is the list of names and addresses. The customers you are looking for will influence the list you select. If you need to get at people, the telephone directory is a useful start, but only 85 per cent of households have phones, so you won't cover all homes; and some areas have a higher ownership of phones than others. Nevertheless, it's a start. A better source would be the electoral registers which may be inspected at the local library.

If you want to contact buyers in factories, use the Yellow Pages and the various trade directories of companies in particular trades, which can also be inspected at the local library. List brokers will supply you, at a cost, with a list as narrowly defined as you wish, but a few hours spent in your reference library, using the photocopying service usually available, is the simplest way for a small company to build a list.

Plan your direct mail as a campaign. To send just one shot is usually inadequate because people don't respond very quickly. Don't collect hundreds of names and send them all the same letter: your returns are likely to be nil. No matter how good you think your letter is, it is only as good as the results it achieves.

Start with a number of potential customers, conveniently located so you could easily visit them. The number you consider reasonable should reflect the nature of the product or service you are marketing.

A gardening service to householders might need a list of twenty-five to start with. A financial and accounting service to retailers could be offered to fifty shops. A design service for companies, perhaps a hundred. A seminar on marketing for the small business, at least 1,000. There are no rules, only an intelligent assessment of each situation.

The direct mail campaign

Prepare, say, three shots in your campaign, linking each shot with the previous one. If you want a good lesson in campaign planning, write for details of some of the products and services you see advertised, particularly organizations offering to teach you something. Naturally it would be invidious in this guide to name any particular advertisers, but some continue to press for a response with several follow-up shots. Each time the message is more urgent: the second shot usually contains a privilege voucher with a cash deduction for immediate action; the third shot often provides further evidence from satisfied customers. Each time there is no time to lose!

These advertisers are very experienced in direct mail, and know the percentage that will buy after each shot. They construct their campaign to suit their target market.

The direct mail letter

Few people throw away unopened envelopes even if they know that the contents are 'just another circular!' So you have just a few seconds to get the attention of the recipient before an initial judgment is made. This must be your first objective: to gain the prospect's attention. We consider a direct mail shot from the view-point of the receiver.

Envelope

White envelopes (22 cm×11 cm) are preferable to brown, which should only be used for large packs of paper or samples. An attractive stamp will gain more attention than a machine stamping. For unusual stamping of a special mailing, have your mail posted from overseas. Luxembourg, for example, has regular issues of attractive stamps, and currently it's cheaper to post from there to the UK than from within the UK itself.

Letter-heading

Use simple, good quality white paper with single-colour printing, preferably black. If you opt for something other than black printing on plain white paper, you'll regret the cost of special continuation paper and envelopes.

Who you are, your address and telephone number should be

neatly printed at the top so that it can be easily read. Clarity should have precedence over design and layout.

If you are a specialist and will continue to specialize, your business, trade or profession may be printed below your name. On balance, it is better to omit it because it is restrictive. You can always have it emblazoned on your sales literature, price list etc.

Folding of contents

It should be easy for the receiver to remove the contents from the envelope. If there are a number of enclosures, they should be folded the same way to avoid having to shuffle them around before they can be read. If you do the inserting yourself, it's easy; if you have to rely on others, make sure they are adequately instructed.

The proposition

Mail to people who will be interested in your proposition; it's no use offering a gardening service to people living in high-rise apartments. Write in the language of the recipients, in the way you would talk to them. Enclose sufficient data in the envelope to make it easy for the receiver to understand what you are offering, and how much it will cost.

Don't offer a product or a service; offer benefits. No one buys a product for itself alone, but for the satisfaction it provides. Offer benefits in your letter to create desire.

The letter, enclosures and your proposition must be convincing and believable. If you have testimonials or references available, use them. A third-party reference is a powerful ally in selling. Guarantee absolute satisfaction or money is refunded, or no invoice is submitted, whichever is appropriate.

Make full use of the weight allowed by the postage you are paying. If relevant, enclose a full-colour leaflet. These can be obtained at very low prices from specialist printers who frequently advertise in the classified columns of the Sunday papers.

Photograph

Photographs are useful for direct mail and also news releases. If you use one, have the caption or full description typed on a separate piece of paper and fixed to the back with suitable paste. If you want to damage the photo, write on the reverse with a ball-point pen, and press hard! Enclose letter and photo in a stiff cardboard-reinforced envelope, with a warning on the front that it contains a photograph.

Action

The recipient should know what has to be done to obtain the product or service. Make it easy: enclose an order form or card that only needs indicating in appropriate squares. On a small mailing, of up to thirty or so, it's worth enclosing an addressed envelope. If your proposition is substantial, it may even be worth while doubling your postage and enclosing a stamped addressed envelope. The Post Office Freepost service should only be used for large mailings.

Composing the letter

Writing is for reading! Therefore, whatever you write, read; and read it aloud. Does it flow? Do you like it? Do you understand it? If you have to write your own direct mail letter, you can't just sit down and expect to write it in one go. It's like carving a wooden statue: you start with a crude lump and gradually refine it.

Compose your letters in a bound book and don't tear out the pages. Don't worry about how to start: just write something such as, 'I am trying to write to people to sell my . . . ' When you're stuck, turn over the page and start again.

A plain, simple letter stating what you are offering, what it will cost and how the receiver can obtain it is better than a post-box full of contrived gimmicks. However, if you can learn to sell in your direct mail shots, they will create more interest, and you stand a greater chance of making a sale.

Let us assume that you are writing to householders offering your gardening service. Exhibit 6.4 is a first attempt.

If you have a person's name, use it and end with 'Yours sincerely', instead of 'Dear Sir', or 'Dear Madam', and 'Yours faithfully'. Never use, 'Dear Sir or Madam'. The first paragraph of the exhibit is in an old-fashioned style and should not be used. Each paragraph starts with 'I': avoid this by rewording. Mr Goodfellow would be

---

JOHN GARDNER

Acorn Cottage · Oak Lane · Croydon · Surrey · CR1 2XY
Tel: 01–234 5678

12 Sep 1989

Mr. James Goodfellow
Hazledean
Coppice Lane,
Reigate Surrey,
GU1 23A

Dear Sir

I am taking this opportunity of notifying you of the gardening services I can offer.

I have a degree in horticulture from London, Wye College and my experience has been with Camelots of Reading for ten years.

I am fully equipped and am able to provide you with excellent weekly maintenance of your garden at reasonable rates.

I look forward to hearing from you and enclose an addressed envelope for your reply.

Yours faithfully

John Gardner

Exhibit 6.4 Direct mail letter – first draft

more interested in what he can get – write 'you' more often than 'I'. The letter has the merit of simplicity but it doesn't exactly zing. Let's improve it, taking these points into consideration. Exhibit 6.5 is the second draft.

Notice the absence of punctuation in the date and the address, and how, apart from the date, everything is lined up on the left-hand side. This is a more up-to-date style of presentation.

JOHN GARDNER

Acorn Cottage · Oak Lane · Croydon · Surrey · CR1 2XY
Tel: 01–234 5678

12 Sep 1989

Mr James Goodfellow
Hazledean
Coppice Lane
Reigate Surrey
GU1 23A

Dear Mr Goodfellow

There are many jobs in the garden where an extra pair of hands or
the advice of an experienced gardener would be invaluable.

I offer such a service and have all the necessary machinery and
equipment. For ten years, before I started my own business, I was
with Camelots of Reading, the leading horticulturists in the south
of England. Before that I spent four years at Wye College,
studying.

My present clients have several different arrangements with me,
ranging from the occasional day to regular weekly maintenance.

If you are interested and would like to discuss this, please give me
a ring. I am sure that you would find my rates as attractive as my
work.

Yours sincerely

John Gardner

Exhibit 6.5 Direct mail letter – second draft

Because of the type of service you are offering, it may be better to
ask the prospect to phone you. You could also enclose an addressed
envelope, and end the letter by saying, 'Please drop me a line, or
phone me when convenient.'

The last paragraph needs pruning. If Mr Goodfellow is interested, of course he will need to discuss it. It should read:

If you are interested, please give me a ring. I am sure that you would find my rates as attractive as my work.

Or if you think you should include an addressed envelope:

If you are interested, please let me know or, better still, give me a ring. I am sure that you would find my rates as attractive as my work.

If you consider that a stamped addressed envelope would be better for your particular operation:

If you are interested, please let me know; a stamped addressed envelope is enclosed for your use. If you prefer, why not give me a ring?

I am sure that you would find my rates as attractive as my work.

The letter is improved, but one letter does not make a campaign. A second letter should be sent to those people who have not responded. This could deal with your rates and is shown in exhibit 6.6.

It is natural to feel that you are worrying people or are a nuisance when you start trying to sell your products and services. Suppress such thoughts. Successful business is built on ideas, inventions, flair and luck, but, above all, on sheer, persistent tenacity. Don't be put off by the first 'No'. Don't be upset if you hear nothing. Keep pressing on.

Consider how a child asks its mother for something. 'Mummy, can I have one?' 'Eh?' 'Can I mum?' 'Please?' 'Mummy . . . can I?' 'M-u-mm-eeey!' 'Why can't I?' 'Oh! Please mummy.' 'David has one!' 'Mummy!'

Children do not stop trying after receiving the first 'No'. Neither should you. So with no response to the second letter, we send a third as in exhibit 6.7.

An industrial product letter

In chapter 3 the potential market for a shower-head was discussed. Three direct mail shots were planned but the response from the first was so high that the other two were cancelled. The tenor of the

---

JOHN GARDNER

Acorn Cottage · Oak Lane · Croydon · Surrey · CR1 2XY
Tel: 01–234 5678

22 Sep 1989

Mr James Goodfellow
Hazledean
Coppice Lane
Reigate Surrey
GU1 23A

Dear Mr Goodfellow

I am wondering whether you have had the opportunity of considering the letter I sent you recently on the gardening services I can offer.

A number of people have already asked me to work for them. If you are thinking of using my services, please let me know soon. Some comments from people for whom I work are enclosed.

For your information, I have also enclosed a copy of my current rates.

Yours sincerely

John Gardner

Exhibit 6.6 A second shot

replies required a form follow-up letter instead. The first shot and form letter are shown in exhibits 6.8 and 6.9.

Direct mail gimmicks

You must be careful with gimmicks. Unless they are well done, they have the opposite of the effect desired, and can erect a barrier between you and the recipients. In general it is better to send plain

---

JOHN GARDNER

Acorn Cottage · Oak Lane · Croydon · Surrey CR1 2XY
Tel: 01–234 5678

Mr James Goodfellow   22 Oct 1989
Hazledean
Coppice Lane
Reigate Surrey
GU1 23A

Dear Mr Goodfellow

Last week I helped one of my clients to gather the fruits of last year's
efforts. He has a modest-size garden but we picked sufficient produce to see
his family through the winter.

During the week I also prepared a new layout for another client who has
just taken over a large garden that has been allowed to grow wild. We will
be putting down new paths, and planting a range of attractive shrubs as
from next week.

Meanwhile I am keeping my other clients' gardens in good order, and
reducing the amount of physical effort they need to expend.

I hope that I can be of service to you and look forward to hearing from you.

Yours sincerely

John Gardner

Exhibit 6.7 A third shot

letters, as short as possible yet containing all the necessary data. One
that was used in 1988 by a company in Wokingham, Berks, illustrates
the kind of gimmick that can be used once, by a small or large
company.

The company purchased several hundred good quality handker-
chiefs and mailed them with a letter to prospects. The objective of

---

2 Aug 1988

Dear Sirs

We have developed a turbo-flow shower-head that provides similar jet
characteristics to ordinary shower-heads but with much reduced water
flow.

The saving in water usage is in the region of 50 per cent. Shower
installations with instant electrical water heating show a reduction in
energy consumption of around 40 per cent.

A heater that normally takes, say, 9 kW, only requires 4 kW. The shower-
head can be fitted to all types of equipment, and is patented throughout
Europe and the USA.

If you are interested in considering the adoption of this head, I will be
pleased to supply further details and arrange for a sample head for you to
test.

Yours faithfully

Exhibit 6.8 Direct mail shot for shower-head

the mailing was to open doors for the company's sales people. The
letter explained that the enclosed handkerchief was not an ordinary
one but would show an interesting message if they *looked at it in the
right light*. The words in italics were used in the letter. The double
meaning was not lost on recipients.

Various types of light were undoubtedly tried on the handkerchief
without result. However, doors that had previously been closed to
the company were opened. The sales people did not refer to the
handkerchief unless they were asked. The only recipient who didn't
ask was a newly recruited buyer who had not seen the mailing.

The sales person would take from a briefcase what looked like a
medium-sized torch, and ask the buyer to hold up the handkerchief
by its corners at arms length. The 'torch', a portable projector, was
switched on. On the handkerchief appeared a message that could be
read by the buyer, announcing a new, greatly improved product
being offered at a low introductory price.

2 Sep 1988

Dear Mr Prospect

Further to our recent correspondence, I have arranged for a shower-head to be sent to you direct from our development works at Pilning, Bristol, UK.

We are finalizing the details of the moulds, and for the moment the heads are individually machined. There has been a great interest in them, resulting in an overwhelming request for samples.

A sample head is on its way to you. When you have had the opportunity of testing it, we can discuss the variations possible in design geometry to provide a shower pattern you consider suitable for your market.

Yours sincerely

Exhibit 6.9 Follow-up form letter for shower-head

The point is that with such a gimmick there must be a bonus in it for the buyer, otherwise the gimmick is an end in itself. No information on the new product had previously been circulated to the buyer, and the sales people were armed not only with the portable projector but also with full literature on the product and a sample for trial. The conversion rate was extremely high.

Monitoring results

Keep an eye on the responses to your direct mail efforts with a simple analysis of each shot and the total campaign. The specimen form in exhibit 6.10 is for three shots for the gardening service. This analysis shows that a profit is not always made after the first shot, but often takes another two or three.

The figure that indicates the effectiveness of the campaign is the

Date sent	Shot 1 12 Sep	Shot 2 22 Sep	Shot 3 22 Oct
Number sent	25	22	18
Production cost (£)	50.00	2.00	2.00
Postage (£)	4.75	4.18	3.42
Total cost (£)	54.75	6.18	5.42
Cumulative cost (£)	54.75	60.93	66.35
Unit cost (£)	2.19	0.28	0.30
No. of replies	3	4	2
Response to shot	12%	18%	11%
Total replies	3	7	9
Average cost of lead (£)	18.25	8.70	7.37
No. orders recd.	2	2	3
Cumulative orders received	2	4	7
Value of orders (£)	30.00	30.00	45.00
Cumulative revenue (£)	30.00	60.00	105.00
Cumulative cost per order (£)	27.38	15.23	9.48
Profit of shot (£)	(24.75)	23.82	39.58
Cumulative gross profit (£)	(24.75)	(0.93)	38.65

Exhibit 6.10 Monitoring direct mail results

average cost per reply. As you can see from the analysis, the cost of replies falls from just over £18 with the first shot to just over £7 with the third. With successive campaigns you will be able to determine the average cost of getting a reply from your efforts.

If prospects are able to send orders, the form is extended to include an analysis of these. After the third shot, the cumulative gross profit is £38.65 on a sales turnover of £105, which is nearly 37 per cent. If a fourth shot were sent at a cost of, say, £5, and no orders were received, the profit percentage would fall to 32 per cent.

Monitoring results of direct mail in this way helps you with decision-making, and not only maintains control of costs, but gives a running profit figure and indicates what type of letters pull. This may be done manually with a calculator or put on a personal computer.

Sales literature

As with a direct mail campaign, before you start, decide what the sales literature is going to be used for. It may be for use by the sales people, for door-to-door circularizing, to be given to visitors, sent by post to enquirers, included in the packing of other products, and so on. When you are clear on its uses, this will influence its design and message.

A small business can afford to have sales literature. The simplest way is to have it prepared on a personal computer, printed by laser, and photocopied as the need arises. More elaborate are the specialist printers who will print a few thousand four-colour A4-size leaflets for £200 or so.

Your best guide is the sales literature of other successful companies. However, you may find that what you like is not what you can afford! Nevertheless, keep samples in a file for future reference.

There are three stages in the preparation of sales literature: design and layout; production of the artwork, such as photographs, transparencies, drawings, typesetting; and printing. Cost of printing is usually straightforward, and if you ask different printers for a price of a given quantity printed in a certain number of colours, with artwork supplied, you will receive similar quotations.

Ask at least three different printers to quote because sometimes some of them need the work and are prepared to trim their price to get it. Also, if it's simple, it can be printed by an apprentice.

Using an advertising agency can be an expensive business for a small company. It is better to use the services of free-lance designers who are also able to prepare the artwork. Printers can usually point you in the right direction.

When you see the designer, explain what you want with a rough pencil outline, or with an example from another company. Ask what the fee will be for the design and layout before you say 'Yes'. And, still before you say 'Yes', ask for an estimate for the artwork for the proposed design. If you think the price is high, ask why, and how it could be reduced. When commissioning sales literature and buying print, find out how much it is likely to be *before you agree to proceed*.

As an example, it is possible to buy 5,000 A4-size four-colour leaflets printed one side for between £200 and £300. But if you have more than one colour photograph, or require a layout different from the standard offered by the printers, the cost can be tripled and even quadrupled.

Headline

The headline should announce what the product or service does for the user. Here are some examples:

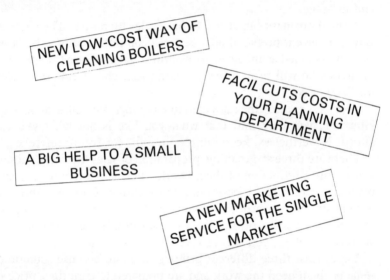

Use the headline to signal your target audience. That is, make it clear to whom you are appealing: retailers, cafés, chemists, engineers, gardeners, golfers etc.

Long headlines are acceptable if they are factual, contain a benefit and are aimed at the target audience. However, avoid negative headlines.

Illustration

Link the illustration with the headline and use a photograph in preference to a drawing. Show the product or service in use, or the results of its having been used. If your service or product improves something, show 'before' and 'after' illustrations. Always have a caption for an illustration.

Body matter

Make the message as simple and short as possible. Keep in mind the objective of the literature. The layout should be clean, making it easy to read and understand the text. Check the spelling. If the matter is prepared on a personal computer with a standard word processing package, this should sort out misspellings such as, 'accomodation' and 'seperate', but it will fail to pick up such errors as: 'The *principle* buyers of the independent retailer were in *there* offices.' Have your text checked by a competent authority before it is given to the printer.

Double-check dates, addresses, telephone numbers and all important facts; read them out to a fearless friend.

Display advertising

Display advertisements are much more costly than classified ads and will probably not interest the small business until turnover is substantial. To insert a single display ad is a waste of money; advertising is only effective when it is maintained continuously.

Display advertisements are sometimes grouped together on a page, and sometimes with the editorial matter of the publication. If you stipulate such a special position or particular page, the cost is higher and relative to the position. Ads with no special position are inserted where convenient for the make-up of the paper and termed 'run-of-paper' (ROP).

Display ads are bought in multiples of single column centimetres (abbreviated to SCC). Typical sizes are shown in exhibit 6.11. If the SCC rate is, say, £2, the four ads would cost respectively £20, £60, £120 and £320.

A display advertisement requires a layout – showing positions of wording and illustration. The preparation of this is called *production* of the ad, and can be costly depending on the quality you wish to achieve.

You do not have time to study all the intricacies of advertising and printing; leave it to the experts, but understand what is involved. To appreciate the standard of display ads, look at recent issues of local newspapers for local businesses. Ignore national names: their

Size	Name	Single column centimetres (SCC)
10 cm × 1 column	10 cm single	10
15 cm × 2 columns	15 cm double	30
20 cm × 3 columns	20 cm triple	60
32 cm × 5 columns	32 cm across five	160

Exhibit 6.11 Common sizes of display advertisements

ads are centrally prepared to a high standard and copies sent to the papers for local insertion. Look at local store advertising, and you will have an idea of what can be achieved for you by the local paper.

What size and how often?

A question often posed is, 'How many people will notice an advertisement?' And not only notice it, but how many times do they need to see it before they act on it? The question of size is not relevant for classified advertising: you just keep advertising regularly. When you are ready to place display advertisements, the situation is more complicated. The size and position of the ad will influence the number of people who see it. It is difficult to miss a whole-page advertisement, and most readers will be aware of it. But this does not mean it will be read.

Research over many years indicates that, in general, about 20 per cent of readers of a publication will notice a particular advert if it is a reasonable size. This 'reasonable' size is relative to the page size. Exhibit 6.12 gives the sizes of advertisement that are considered to have similar attention value.

If about 20 per cent of readers notice the ad, it would seem that an ad needs to be inserted at least five times before there is a chance of all seeing it. But the situation is not that simple. The 20 per cent of readers who notice it each time it appears won't be a different 20 per cent. If it appears, say, five times, some readers will see it twice, some three times and so on. About ten insertions are necessary for

Size of publication	Comparable size of ad
Tabloid papers (e.g. Sun, Mail, Mirror)	15 cm double column
Broadsheet (e.g. Times, Telegraph)	20 cm triple column
Large periodicals	quarter page
Small periodicals	half page
Pocket magazines	whole page (WP)

Exhibit 6.12 Comparable attention sizes

an ad to have good exposure and a chance of being seen by the majority of readers.

To have an advert in a broadsheet paper with the same attention value as an ad in a tabloid, the size has to be doubled – from 30 column centimetres to 60 column centimetres. These two sizes are in proportion, as is a 32 cm across five columns. This is important when considering production costs. You need only one piece of artwork prepared for the largest size: it is easily reduced in proportion to fit the other two.

Comparing costs

Comparing costs of classified ads is fairly simple. Calculate the cost of, say, six lines in each paper and compare costs with the circulations of the papers.

For display advertising, costs of different media can be compared by bearing in mind the 'comparable attention size' advertisements and the estimate that 20 per cent of readers notice the ad. The formula is:

$$\frac{\text{Cost of comparable size advertisement}}{20 \text{ per cent of thousands of readers}}$$

'Circulation' may be substituted for 'readers' in this formula since readership figures are based on certified circulation, and are calculated by means of surveys and statistical forecasting. To illustrate the use of the formula, and compare costs of display advertising in some of the leading newspapers, exhibit 6.13 is based on circulation and readership data for 1989.

Publication	Circulation (× 1,000)	Readers (×1,000)	SCC	15 cm double	20 cm triple	Cost per Circulation 20%	1,000 Readers 20%
Daily Express	1,679	4,306	£85	£2,550	–	£7.59	£2.96
Daily Mail	1,793	4,531	£82	£2,460	–	£6.86	£2.71
Sun	4,147	11,340	£99	£2,970	–	£3.58	£1.31
The Times	450	1,213	£29	–	£1,740	£19.33	£7.17
Daily Telegraph	1,139	2,765	£58	–	£3,480	£15.28	£6.29
Sunday Times	1,363	3,641	£72	–	£4,320	£15.84	£5.93
Sunday Telegraph	716	2,163	£42	–	£2,520	£17.60	£5.83
News of the World	5,214	12,808	£105	–	£6,300	£6.04	£2.46

Exhibit 6.13 Media comparisons

The advertising plan

Before you can prepare a plan for advertising, you should have a general marketing plan. This must cover what type of product you intend to market; what prices you are prepared to accept from what target market; and what are your sales and profit expectations. We shall consider the subject of planning in chapter 10.

Key points

- Define your target audience and make your appeals to them.
- Emphasize the unique *buying* points of your product or service.
- Concentrate your early promotion to a convenient area near to your base of operations.
- Direct mail is the most powerful method of getting to your prospective customers, but monitor results.
- Use simply produced sales literature and price lists.

7

Promotion

Outline

There are other ways in which you can stimulate the sale of your product or service than by advertising and personal selling. We look at:

- price cuts
- price tickets
- stuffers
- instructions
- press releases
- a sale
- point-of-sale
- displays
- business gifts
- exhibitions
- coupons and vouchers
- multi-packs
- packaging
- reusable containers

Flexibility of promotion

There are two main ways that products and services may be distributed: they can be pushed through the channel or pulled through the channel. *Pushing through the channel* requires pressure on the middlemen – the wholesalers and retailers or stockists – with personal selling, advertising and promotion. *Pulling through the channel* is promoting the product or service to ultimate users with the object of persuading them to purchase it at convenient outlets.

Both push and pull strategies can be adopted by companies on a long-term basis in terms of years, or on a short-term basis of, say, a month or less.

Long-term push requires a company to build up its sales organization and connections with trade channels to achieve an extensive market coverage. It needs continuous investment.

The most expensive is long-term pull. It implies that a large volume of publicity is maintained and is not something that can be quickly decided and implemented. The object of long-term pull is to develop the *image* of the product over many years so that there is a high level of brand or product awareness in the market. It is big company strategy.

In contrast, short-term push or pull can be used at any time, and can be as simple as offering a price reduction to the middleman or the consumer during a slack month. It is ideal for the small business. Because of its flexibility, a lot of promotion can be turned on and off like a tap, and most of the techniques applied to both distributors and ultimate users. All are used in the short term.

The suggestions listed in the aims of the chapter have been graded in approximate order of cost and importance to a small business.

Price cuts

A price cut can be offered to distributor or user. *It should only be used in an attempt to achieve a express objective.* Price cutting without some reasonable, attainable objective is a short-sighted technique for giving away some of your profit. While you do not have to lay out any cash for this form of promotion, it costs you some of your *unit profit*. The word 'unit', is important. When you cut price you always reduce your unit profit; you may or may not increase your *total profit*. Turnover may increase as a result of cutting price, but what keeps your business afloat is profit, not turnover.

The effect on your total profit will depend how many more you sell as a consequence of the price cut. As you will have read in chapter 4, if your product has an elastic demand, cutting the price by, say, 10 per cent will normally increase sales by more than 10 per cent. Suppose you have a product with an elastic demand: a price cut of 10 per cent causes sales to increase by 20 per cent. Such a situation could be as shown in exhibit 7.1.

Price	Unit profit	Sales	Turnover	Total profit
£20	£7	100	£2,000	£700
£18	£5	120	£2,160	£600

Exhibit 7.1 Price cut with an elastic demand

If unit profit is normally £7 on a product sold at £20, cutting the price to £18 reduces unit profit to £5. With sales at one hundred the total profit is £700; as a result of the 10 per cent price cut, although sales increase by 20 per cent, the total profit is reduced to £600.

The number that needs to be sold at the proposed reduced price to improve the total profit figure is a simple calculation. Decide the improved total profit desired – say, £900. Divide this figure by the unit profit: 900/5 = 180. This represents an 80 per cent increase in sales.

You could also conjecture what might happen by *increasing* the price rather than cutting it by 10 per cent. If sales fell by 20 per cent, the situation would be as shown in exhibit 7.2.

Price	Unit profit	Sales	Turnover	Total profit
£20	£7	100	£2,000	£700
£22	£9	80	£1,760	£720

Exhibit 7.2 Price increase with an elastic demand

While a price cut will generally promote sales, if it can result in a reduction of your total profit, you must be clear on the objective for adopting it. There are two indicators to consider: the degree of need of the product and the frequency of purchase.

Price may be important if the need for the product is high. But some need products, such as food, are purchased every day; other need products, such as beds, are purchased infrequently, and a price cut may not be a promotional stimulus.

You should also consider the likelihood of competitive responses to your price cut. If it results in a deeper cut by your competitor, you can either re-cut or stay with your reduced price. The net effect is that you and your competitors sacrifice profit.

If the product or service is purchased very infrequently, a price cut that stimulates increased sales would prevent competitors from selling some of their products. Beyond the fact that a price cut always reduces unit profit, it is not possible to generalize: each situation must be thoroughly assessed before the cut is made. If your product is currently on sale at retailer or stockists, a price cut also has to be made for the existing stock. Middlemen do not welcome a reduction in their margins, so an allowance will have to be made.

Here are some reasons, roughly in order of merit, when a price cut could be considered as an acceptable and reasonable marketing tactic:

- to obtain publicity, especially with a new product (a limit should be placed on the number offered at the reduced price);
- to launch a new product on the market and gain speedy penetration;
- to clear current stocks held by stockists;
- to attract customers to the premises where they are able to purchase other, more profitable products;
- to counter a competitor's new product launch or otherwise create problems for them;
- to generate cash and reduce stock (especially before annual stock-taking);
- to increase market share;
- to combat a competitor's price reduction.

Price tickets

Price tickets on products are sometimes elusive and sometimes cannot be distinguished from other figures such as the date of manufacture, equivalent continental size, sell-by date, fabric number, packer's number etc. If you want to sell your product and it is appropriate to carry a price ticket, make it easy to see. If VAT is in-cluded, say so on the ticket. If price is net-of-tax because it is subject to discount, clearly state this on the price ticket.

A poorly presented price ticket quickly lowers the image of the product. It is not necessary to have expensively produced price tickets, but they must be well prepared and of uniform standard. If you have a company design or logo, this should be incorporated in the design of the price ticket. The price information should be of a size comparable with the product; small products having comparat-ively small tickets, large products with larger, but not enormous tickets. All prices should be readable from the normal viewing distance.

If you have a window or other display of a number of products, they could be displayed in price ranges: different coloured price tickets might be used to indicate the different groups of prices.

Stuffers

One of the simplest forms of promotion is to 'stuff' your mail and all product packaging with information on your products in the form of small printed leaflets – 'stuffers'. Every time you mail an envelope containing a letter, invoice, statement, acknowledgement etc., you should use the maximum weight of postage the stamp permits.

Leaflets have an advantage over folders: they can be held and inspected with one hand. Stuffers do not need to be expensively printed but they should be well-designed and produced. If you have a range of products or styles, or different services, you should have at least one stuffer for each. If you have only one product or service, then you could illustrate a series of situations where your product or service can be used.

Consider John Gardner's gardening service. He could arrange to have photographs taken of different gardens he has prepared and any special features installed. Also of interest would be a series of spring, summer, autumn and winter gardening hints, information on fertilizers and pest controls.

The issue of stuffers must be controlled to ensure that they are topical, and that all recipients receive the same promotional material. Strive for unity in promotion. What is included in the mail and other packing in any one period should be reflected in the direct mail, advertising, display and other publicity. Concentrating the message on one theme at a time will achieve the maximum impact.

As business develops and the product range is extended, undoubtedly you will have descriptive, illustrated sales literature designed. A modified leaflet should be prepared for stuffers.

User instructions

Where the small business can score over larger competitors is in its ability to give customer service. Many products need detailed instructions for their assembly, directions for use, advice for best results, guide to cleaning, explanation of how they work etc.

Give a lot of thought to this aspect of promotion. Even if you are selling a product that already contains the original manufacturer's instructions, consider the value of expanding these. Even large multinational producers of products are not immune from inconsistencies and 'bugs' in their instructions.

A well-known baking product provides instructions on the preparation of the product: towards the end of these explicit directions the cook is told to place the prepared mix in a warm dish. There is a short pause while another pair of hands has to obtain the dish and warm it! Obviously, the instructions should have started with: 'Warm a 10-inch dish . . . '

This is similar to the annoying habit of people who used to dictate letters for typing on recording machines before photocopiers and word processors were available. At the end of the dictation they would add, 'Take an extra carbon copy of this please.'

If it is possible, prepare your own instructions and advice for the customer to obtain the maximum benefit from using the product. Have the instructions reproduced on paper with your name or logo so that it is easily identified as having been issued by your business.

Press releases

Details about your products and services can appear in the press in two main ways: advertising and editorial mention. You have to pay for advertising, but editorial matter is at the discretion of the editor. The vast majority of editorial content of trade magazines is prepared from press releases, also called news releases, received by the publication. The essential requirement is that it must be *news*.

An example of a press release that is unlikely to be used is given in exhibit 7.3. It is true; it states the bald facts; but it is not news. People are offering services every day. It will be 'spiked' in the editorial office; that is, stuck onto a metal spike with many others and eventually dumped.

NEWS RELEASE

John Gardner, BSc (Horticulture) is offering a complete gardening service to householders in the Croydon and district area.

After obtaining his degree from London University, Wye College, he spent ten years with Camelots at Reading.

He has all the necessary equipment and transport and provides a weekly maintenance in addition to complete garden layouts for clients.

He can be contacted on 01–234 5678.

Exhibit 7.3 Example of a non-news release

Imagine an airline sending out a press release which announces that one of its planes has landed safely at Heathrow. This is not news; it is happening every few minutes, every day.

But a plane with part of its fuselage missing landing safely *is* news, and so newsworthy that it would not be the subject of a press release but of phone calls. The subsequent investigation and explanation for the incident would, of course, be an appropriate topic for a news release.

You might ask: when is it *news*? It is news when it is:

- confidential, or – better still – secret;

- confounding common sense;
- directly important to a lot of people;
- funny for everyone;
- involving conflict;
- mysterious or bewildering;
- new (i.e. it has not happened previously);
- novel (i.e. it's not new, but completely different);
- relating to famous people or places;
- romantic enough to capture people's imagination.

This is not a definitive list of what makes news, but what is of general interest to editors. The example in exhibit 7.3 falls into none of these categories. News is of two main types: an event that occurs; an event that is constructed, arranged, or contrived.

Consider the geographic area of interest that a news item might affect, and the extent to which media cover that area. An item of purely local news will not interest a national newspaper. But something of interest to the whole country, even if it concerns a small locality, would be of interest to a national paper, and would be wasted if offered to the local newspaper.

For the small business, here is an alphabetical selection of items that could be arranged and be subjects of one or more news releases:

- Announce an election to be held.
- Announce names of a committee.
- Announce praise for something or someone.
- Arrange a demonstration.
- Celebrate an appropriate anniversary.
- Conduct a poll or survey.
- Entertain well-known or appropriate people.
- Hold a contest.
- Interview a national or local celebrity.
- Issue a protest.
- Issue a summary of relevant facts.
- Issue an analysis of a relevant topic.
- Make a prediction.
- Make a trip of unusual interest.
- Organize a tour.
- Organize a trade promotion.
- Participate in an important local issue.

- Present an award.
- Publish a report.
- Publish a testimonial from a well-known person.
- Publish an appointment.
- Release a letter received from a well-known person.
- Stage a debate.
- Stage a special event.
- Tie-in with a holiday.
- Tie-in with a special day or week.
- Tie-in with another publicity effort.
- Tie-in with news events of the day.
- Tie-in with other media on a mutually interesting project.
- Write a letter to the editor.

None of the above items just happens: they have to be worked at. Some that might be adapted for John Gardner's gardening service are:

- Interviews could be arranged with well-known local persons on the subject of their gardens.
- A demonstration of gardening techniques could be organized, and the event announced in a release.
- John Gardner could prepare an analysis of local gardening problems with suggestions on how to deal with them.
- He might be able to obtain a testimonial from a well-known person for whom he works and use this in a news release.
- He could arrange a tie-in with another publicity effort related to gardening.
- He could write a letter to the editor on either a local topic or one that he considers would have wide interest.

For the small business as well as the big organization, the value of being mentioned in editorial columns of publications is continuity. It is the occasional, but regular little tap of publicity that develops the image in the mind of the general public and target audience.

If you prepare a news release, use the following guidelines. They are not rules but points that will help your release to gain the attention of the editor.

- Double-space the release; if it is very short, use triple-spacing. Leave wide margins for notes to be added by the editor.

- Add a suitable headline only if it will help to 'sell' the item to the editor.
- Use a bold heading of 'NEWS RELEASE' or 'PRESS RELEASE'. Your name, company or the person issuing it should appear on the second line.
- Set the date of issue prominently at the top. Don't use 'Immediate': it's old-fashioned and doesn't indicate the date. Some organizations, particularly government departments, issue press releases to many different types of media, dailies, weeklies etc., and sometimes give a forward date on which the news can be published.
- Do not indent the first paragraph. Newspapers, books and magazines all follow this convention, so it gives a professional look to the layout.
- In the first paragraph state: *who, what, when, where, how* and *why*. Be severely accurate, but get your name or business in the first paragraph or as high as possible in the release. All publications are short of space; if your release is used, it may be cut to only the first paragraph.
- State simple, straightforward facts in an objective style. Sentences should preferably be short. There should be no opinions or comment, except from a well-known person. Avoid the use of adjectives, coloured words and conclusions unless they appear in a direct quotation from an important source.
- If there is more than one page, insert 'more' at the bottom of each and 'ends' at the bottom of the last page.
- Consider the day of publication of media when sending out releases. If your local paper is published on a Friday, make sure they have your item by Tuesday. A monthly trade magazine should receive the release immediately after the previous issue is published.

Exhibit 7.4 is a general layout for a one-page release. Exhibit 7.5 is a rewrite of exhibit 7.3. It is to be sent to the local paper, but should not be considered as the final effort. For example, you might use a line from the second paragraph as the headline: 'John's business is growing!' A lot will depend on the style of paper: the editor might not like words with two meanings. A strong argument in favour of the present headline is that it relates to the customer.

NEWS RELEASE

Release date:

19 Sep 1989

Use double or even triple-spacing throughout. Start first paragraph without any indentation so that all the text lines up underneath the first word which, in this example, is 'Use'.

Indent the second, and all following paragraphs with a couple of spaces. At the top right-hand side insert the date that the item can be published. Usually, unless there is some serious reason to withhold the information, insert today's date.

At the bottom left- or right-hand side, insert the name and telephone number of person who can provide more information if required. If a continuation sheet is used, insert '. . . more . . .' at the centre bottom of each and at the bottom of last sheet put '. . . E N D S . . .'

. . . E N D S . . .

More information from:

John Gardner 01–234 5678

Exhibit 7.4 Layout for a news release

The sale

A sale is the offer of stock at lower-than-normal prices. It is similar to a price-cutting exercise but is usually for a range of stock rather than for one product. Retailers who offer goods for sale must have had them on sale for a minimum of 28 days at the previous price for it to be a genuine legal sale, or else the goods being offered must be the result of a special purchase.

A sale of fashion products is often held as the period of the fashion nears its end, and, it is usual for stocks of summer and winter goods to be sold off towards the end of summer and winter respectively.

The main differences between a price cut and a sale are the objectives: a price cut is to stimulate sales; a sale is to clear stock. When a sale of goods is started, the normal, expected total profit on those goods should have been made on previous turnover, and they may be sold at reduced prices to make space for new stock.

Point-of-sale

Point-of-sale (POS) promotion is publicity and display at the point where the customer is able to buy. At supermarket check-outs, displays of low-priced goods invite customers to pick them up and add them to the goods already being purchased. Chemists' counters have displays and packs of products appropriate to the season: cough tablets in winter, sun-tan lotion in summer, and so on.

Obviously, such POS material is in the province of big business, but for the small business there are endless possibilities. A counter display, informative literature, posters, testimonials, users' reports, photographs and anything else that promotes the product or service can be placed at the point where the potential customer normally makes the purchase.

If you are selling your product or service through a stockist, before you spend any time and money on POS material, discuss the possibility with a number of them. It is pointless to proceed if stockists will be reluctant to use the material. Retailers and stockists receive POS displays, signs, counter packs, dispensers, catalogues, leaflets etc. from every manufacturer with whom they deal. You

---

NEWS RELEASE

19 September 1989

Less backache for local gardeners

Local gardeners now have someone to do the heavy work in the garden. John Gardner, a product of Wye College and Camelots of Reading, not only does the back-aching work, but provides expert advice.

Backed with the help of the local bank and the Small Firms Centre, John's business is growing!

Recently he planted nearly 1,000 asparagus plants in the morning, felled an aged oak in the afternoon, bedded out some winter plants in the early evening for a local pensioner, and then gave a lecture on autumn jobs in the garden to the local Allotment Society.

More information:

John Gardner 01–234 5678

Exhibit 7.5 Example of a news release

start at a disadvantage, but if your point-of-sale will help the stockist to sell out, you stand a better chance of getting it used.

Displays

The object of having a display is to show the product or the result of using the product, to attract people's interest, or reinforce the product's image. A display can be static or animated, but should, if possible, focus on, demonstrate, or bring out the essential product benefits.

The obvious place to have a display is on your premises. If people visit you in the course of business, have one or more displays of your products in use, or being used.

Letters from satisfied customers, especially well-known companies, should, with their permission, be framed and displayed in the reception area where they can be easily read.

Copies of any literature, photographs, posters etc. should all be considered as possible display material, but take care to avoid clutter and an amateurish look.

Life-size, cut-out mounted photographs of people using your product, while costly, are particularly attractive. When choosing models to use your product, select the appropriate professional model to project your message. For example, if you advertise that your product is light and easy to use, have a slim, slight female figure using it.

Pay particular attention to the lighting of displays and premises. It can be used with great effect to increase their attraction.

If you operate from shop premises, make the most of your window display. It is worth paying for advice from a professional display person rather than attempting it yourself. This is particularly true if your product or service does not readily lend itself to being displayed. As with everything you commission in your business, if you want a professional to advise you, ask for a quote before you give the go-ahead. This can save you some unpleasant surprises, because the cost of display and display design does not come cheap.

Business gifts

Business gifts do not increase sales; they promote the name of the company giving the gift. It is difficult, if not impossible, to think of a gift that has not been made before, and the small business has to compete with the large companies who are able to afford more expensive gifts, and distribute them more widely.

Rather than go to the expense of ordering the minimum quantity of a 'standard' business gift printed with your name, it is better to purchase out-of-the-ordinary products and give them with a specially printed 'With compliments' card. The author has used this success-fully on many occasions.

The most recent example was a thin, solar-powered plastic calcu-lator costing a few pounds, which could be inserted into rings of a personal organizer. It had no name printed on it and was obviously not an advertising gift, so recipients could either use it or give it away – which they didn't! When using it, if asked where it had been obtained, the recipient would mention the name of the donor.

Gifts of bottles of alcoholic drink at Christmas serve little useful purpose, and many business people – especially government officials – are not permitted to receive such favours; any gifts must be obvious advertising material. The hospitality boxes at the social event of the year – Ascot – must wait until you are in the big business league.

Coupons and vouchers

Coupons with a nominal face value are used mainly for repeat-purchase consumer products. They are incorporated into the design of a leaflet for door-to-door distribution, or included in advertise-ments in local newspapers.

In effect, they are a form of price-cutting widely used by the manufacturers of mass-marketed consumer products. The small business should use them for promotional objectives other than price reductions.

A coupon entitling the user to some advantage – such as exchang-ing it for an appropriate gift when buying your product – is comparatively easy to organize. The objective must be clear; offering a coupon that is really a disguised price cut achieves only lower profit.

Similar to coupons are vouchers. These are usually more elaborately printed – often individually numbered – to create a more important image. Trade, technical and consumer magazines make wide use of the voucher or special order form to encourage people to subscribe to them. Some large organizations with flexible but costly laser printing facilities will 'personalize' the voucher by inserting the recipient's name on it and in the body of the letter sent with it. Despite this, the purpose of vouchers is much the same as coupons, but their nominal value is higher.

A coupon would be appropriate for 10p or 20p off the normal price of a small consumer item; a voucher would be used to offer a substantial percentage reduction of a much higher priced product or service. The recipient may claim the entitlement if a purchase or reply is made within a certain period of time.

The number of potential customers must influence the use of coupons and vouchers: anything less than four or five thousand or so would not warrant their expense. It would be better to make the special offer in personal letters to potential customers.

Multi-packs

Multi-packs are several of the same product, or complementary products, being offered at a reduced price. Examples are: three bottles of shampoo taped together for the price of two; eight batteries in a shrink-wrapped pack for the price of seven; hair tonic and a comb taped together for the price of the tonic; garden fertilizer and a pest-control powder banded together and offered at 20 per cent less than when purchased separately.

While the use of multi-packs is a form of price cutting, it has the advantage of getting more of the product into the hands of customers. It is also of use when one of the products is well known, and it is desired to publicize the second by linking it with an accepted product.

Packaging

Packing usually refers to the functional enclosure of a product for transporting and handling. Packaging includes the functional packing, but also takes into consideration the publicity value. The nearer the pack to the ultimate purchaser, the greater is the value of packaging as a promotional aid. Thus packs of detergent when delivered to the retailer are in simple, stout outer cartons. The individual packs displayed in the shop or supermarket are printed in strong, eye-catching colours; the name, pack design, colours, and any slogan, all contribute to the general image of the product. The packing of your product should be considered as a promotional opportunity.

One of the most inexpensive forms of packaging, and yet one that provides ample opportunity for promotion, is the use of header cards. These are colourful printed cards stapled to a stout plastic bag that contains the product. The header card can have a hole, or appropriate shape punched in the middle for hanging on a suitable peg or holder. It is almost do-it-yourself packaging: the bags are purchased by the thousand, cards produced by the local printer, and the products packed by part-time labour.

A very small independent shoe retailer in Ostend has built up an extensive trade for his men's and women's footwear primarily on account of his excellent range of shoes, but also because of his service and packaging. Instead of the ordinary shoe box and paper bag, he uses a stout, double-wall corrugated box in the same deep shade of blue as his shop, sliding-door stock cupboards, carpet, fittings and price tickets. The rectangular box opens with a single flap that covers the short top end and halfway down the long front to take a pair of shoes. A simple, effective plastic clip secures the flap, and a comfortable stout handle at the top makes it easy to carry. No other shoe retailer has anything like the container. It is comparatively expensive, yet his range of good quality shoes is equal to the merchandise in some of the better-known shops in the town, but priced significantly lower. It is tempting to suggest that his high turnover is attributable to the boxes into which he puts customers' shoes, yet his repeat purchase sales are unusually high.

A well-designed, attractive pack should create its own attention value, protect the contents and keep them in good condition in transit. If your product lends itself to good packaging, regard this as a sound promotional tool and a ready-made medium for advertising your product and what it does. However, first comes function, then comes fancy: protect your product first, then publicize it.

Reusable containers

The promotional packing box supplied by the Ostend shoe retailer makes an excellent container for transporting shoes on car journeys. The containers may also be used for purposes completely different from carrying their original contents.

Various food products, especially country specialities, honey, jams and pickles, are sold in attractive pots that can be used in the home after the food has been eaten. A brand of French mustard is supplied in glasses that can subsequently be used as everyday wine glasses. One well-known food-retailing chain sells an excellent matured Stilton cheese around Christmas time in a well-sealed, oven-proof pot with lid. These make superb oven casseroles, pudding bowls or cereal dishes when the last of the Stilton has gone, and a new image for the attractive brown container is created.

No one is going to buy a pair of shoes from a retailer because he supplies them in a handsome reusable box, or a jar of honey from you because the china pot can afterwards be used for trinkets, but a really attractive reusable container might just give you the promotional edge over competitors.

Exhibitions

An exhibition has many possibilities. It can be a private reception in a local hotel room, a small 'By invitation only' show, a trade fair focused on a specific industry, an agricultural show, or a widely publicized and well-attended international event.

The object of participating at an exhibition is to meet as many visiting potential buyers as possible. If you hold your own private exhibition, unless you have something unusually attractive or unique, you will not attract sufficient people to make it a viable venture. If you participate in an organized exhibition, you will be in competition with all similar exhibitors.

Whether or not you should exhibit will depend on the degree to which interest in your product can be stimulated and sales promoted. Except with small, low-priced goods, products are not purchased and taken away from exhibitions. Orders are often placed, but more usually follow-up letters and personal calls are necessary before an actual signed order is obtained. You must have the capability of following-up any enquiries and making sales presentations at the potential buyers' premises.

There are a number of exhibitions suitable for the small business but be clear about your objectives before agreeing to participate. If you are thinking of taking space at a publicly organized exhibition, obtain literature and regulations as early as possible. If it has been held before, obtain the statistics on attendance etc.

Calculate the cost of suitable space, design and construction of the stand, display materials and special literature; the cost of people involved and taken away from their normal jobs; travelling and accommodation expenses. Determine if the expenditure is well within the advertising budget and can be justified.

Contact people who have exhibited previously, and obtain their opinions. Here is a check-list from which to select those points appropriate to your business:

- Decide what you are going to exhibit and the specific objectives you aim to achieve.
- Order power, water or special requirements needed on the stand.
- Order a telephone line for the period of the exhibition.
- Arrange for transportation to and from the exhibition for any equipment, machinery etc.
- Arrange any necessary hotel accommodation.
- If products are to be sold from the stand, order suitable secure storage for them on the stand or somewhere convenient.
- Check that your sales literature is suitable, and that you have a sufficient supply; organize it in good time.
- Check on the availability of samples and give-aways.
- Order equipment, tables, chairs etc. for the stand.
- Decide who is to man the stand; arrange for reliefs.
- Prepare a press release for appropriate publications.

- Organize a photograph of the stand.
- Insure any equipment being exhibited.
- Have an emergency kit for repairs etc.
- Organize a procedure for following-up leads obtained.
- Have an adequate supply of exhibition forms, order books, scrap pads, visiting cards, name badges etc.
- If you are selling from the stand, have a buffer stock that can be obtained at short notice.
- Send invitations to customers and prospects.
- Arrange for your base office to be adequately manned while you are away at the exhibition.
- On the day of the exhibition ensure that you visit all other stands of interest and obtain their literature. Do this early, before they run out of supplies!

After the exhibition:

- Follow-up sales leads immediately.
- Check that all equipment is returned in good condition.
- Check all invoices.

Key points

- Sales promotion is the most flexible publicity tool, and it can be focused on the potential customer.
- When using a price cut as promotion, write down the objective you want to achieve; without an objective, cutting price only cuts profits. Establish that the increased turnover needed to maintain the same total profit is reasonable and attainable.
- 'Need' products and 'desire' products require different types of promotion; be clear as to the degree of need your product will have for its intended market.
- Price tickets, stuffers and instructions for use are all strong but inexpensive promotional aids that can have an impact far in excess of their cost.
- If you intend to issue press releases, do so on a regular basis with everything that could possibly be newsworthy to the paper concerned. Don't prejudge anything; let the editor decide – send it.

8

Selling

Outline

Selling, together with advertising, is the promotion component of the marketing mix. We look at:

- selling activities
- sales people or sales agents?
- stock control
- importance of the sales mix
- commission as promotion
- sales management

Selling is vital to your business

No matter how good your product or service, it will not sell itself. You might sell a few of your product simply because people have heard of it, but sustained turnover and profits will only happen if you keep that vital link with customers by selling.

The selling of your products or services is probably the most important aspect of your business, for without sales you make no profits. As we have seen, there are two main selling situations: customers come to you, or you visit them.

If customers come to you, they are already in a buying frame of mind and expect to be 'served'; that is, they expect to have help in buying.

You can sell your product or service in three main ways:

- face-to-face with a buyer or prospective buyer;
- telephone call to a buyer or prospective buyer;
- mail order advertisement.

The first two require that specific people are approached; the third is a general offer.

Assuming that you are working alone, the easiest is the personal sales presentation. You must be reasonably sure that the person is a prospective buyer, and not waste your time trying to sell to someone who is not. Suppose you travel a fair distance to see a company you think could be a customer, and, during your interview with the buyer, find that they have no need of your product or service. You could have established that by a phone call.

While face-to-face selling is the easiest, using the telephone is the quickest, but requires practice. Selling products and services by telephone is usually done between known parties: the receiver knows, or knows of, the caller and, in general, the product or service being offered.

Pre-selling activities

One of the early difficulties of selling is that you cannot know beforehand if a particular person will buy. This requires a pre-selling activity to establish a list of *suspects*.

Suspects, in the selling sense, are people or companies you believe could buy your product. Suspects can be found everywhere and, depending on what you are selling, will influence where you look.

From chapters 2 and 3 you know the importance of defining your product/market. An analysis similar to that shown in exhibit 3.1 will point you in the right direction to search for suspects. If you arm yourself with the description of your proposed product/market, an hour spent in your local reference library will yield many names, addresses and telephone numbers.

You have to establish if these suspects are *prospects* – that is, prospective buyers. A prospect is a qualified suspect, and the telephone is ideal for qualifying prospects and sales leads.

If in due course you intend to make a personal sales presentation, prepare a list of suspects near to your base. How you qualify a prospective buyer will naturally depend on what you are selling: a fast-food delivery service, free-lance advertising, printing, computer-aided design, security devices will all need different information for qualifying as a prospect.

Qualifying prospects

To determine if a prospect might become a customer, four things have to be established:

- Does the prospect have a need for the product or service?
- Does the prospect know of the likely cost and have a budget to purchase the product or service?
- When is the prospect likely to purchase the product?
- Who takes the decision to purchase?

If you are selling to private persons, you should be able to phone them direct. If you are selling to companies, before you can speak with the person concerned you will usually go through the company switchboard and perhaps a secretary. But you can explore the first question with these introductory conversations. Find out if the company uses products or services similar to yours, and ask who is the best person to talk to. Don't try to get information or interviews by subterfuge, such as saying you are conducting a survey or research. On the other hand, it does not always help to say that you are selling. Say that you are a supplier!

Small businesses are mostly dealing in merchandise of low unit order value or low annual cost, so the question of a company having a budget to purchase your product or service may not arise. A company is not going to budget for a gardening service or for locally-made pizzas for its canteen. It is finding out *how* they purchase such services or products that will be of most help to you.

For example, a company that has flowers and potted plants in its reception hall and other rooms, with a twice-weekly call to tend to them, might place a contract annually. It would be pointless to visit them before getting more information and planning your approach. Several visits will probably be needed before you would be invited to quote.

Some small businesses are selling products that customers budget for. The Holborn computer supplier mentioned in chapter 3 is a small business employing about a dozen people. Their reputation has been built on the reliability and speed of their service: anyone who has ever used a computer will know that back-up and service are crucial. Because of this they are often invited to quote companies.

When qualifying prospects on the phone, they summarize the costs involved for initial purchase, software, training and servicing. The prospect is able to compare this with the available budget.

Many of their prospects have a good idea of the initial investment required but are hazy about other costs, and ignorant of the time required to get a system in operation. Their qualification procedure includes this short briefing, which projects confidence in their ability to satisfy the prospect's needs.

If a customer is proposing to purchase now, he is a red-hot prospect and needs your continued attention. If the purchase is to be made in the next financial year, you have time to develop your approach.

Finally, who takes the decision where to place the order? You may be able ascertain this on the phone, but if the purchase is a major one, there is likely to be a decision-making unit as described in chapter 2. Even minor buying decisions are influenced by people other than the one who signs the order. These degrees of influence cannot be obtained over the phone, and must wait until you have an interview.

Who does the selling?

Until such time that you can employ someone to do your selling, you will have to do it. Because it is your business and your livelihood, you bring a certain urgency and, perhaps, enthusiasm to the task. If you adopt a basic selling formula while you are building your business, you will learn a lot about selling your product which you can pass on to your future sales people.

Many formulae have been developed to guide the sales presentation, but fundamental to good selling practice is realizing that buying and selling are merely different descriptions of the same transaction. Successful sales people are those who help customers to buy.

A selling guide that recognizes this, and can be applied to any selling situation is the following:

- *opening* the sale;
- finding out the prospect's real *need*;
- getting the prospect to *resolve* that need;

- making an *offer* to the prospect;
- helping the prospect to *assess* your offer;
- reaching a *decision* to purchase.

The words in italics are the key words and provide the mnemonic to remember the formula: *O*pening, *N*eed, *R*esolution, *O*ffer, *A*ssessment, *D*ecision. The capital letters spell *ONROAD*, which is what sales people are often described as being – on the road, selling.

Opening the sale

After you have said 'Good morning' or whatever to the prospect, commented on the weather, and exchanged a few pleasantries, you can open the sale. The word 'sale' is used, but frequently no actual sale takes place. It depends on the objective you have set. Here are some non-sales objectives:

- to obtain agreement to send a quotation;
- to arrange to carry out a survey of the customer's factory;
- to get the customer to visit your workshop or factory;
- to arrange an appointment with technical staff;
- to arrange a demonstration at the customer's premises;
- to use a free sample of your work.

A sale is opened in one of two ways: making a statement or asking a question.

Statements should be about your product or service, or directly related to it. Assume that you are John Gardner offering a full garden maintenance service in an interview with the facilities manager of a large company that has just moved into the area.

I can offer you a complete garden maintenance service covering all your needs and including weekly attendance to ensure everything is in order.

Too long. Too much information and too difficult to say with any enthusiasm. Try again.

I can provide you with a complete service for your grounds and gardens, supply all the necessary plants etc., and attend to everything weekly, or as necessary.

Even longer and still difficult to say. Two 'necessaries' are unnecessary.

A sales opening is as important as the first few words a speaker utters on getting up and addressing an audience. They must be short, distinct, easy to understand and easy to say. Therefore you should practice aloud with stresses on different words to get the right meaning and projection.

I can offer a complete garden service.

Now it's too short, but the message is clear.

I provide a complete service for the maintenance of grounds and gardens throughout the district.

Better. But the service may be mainly for small domestic gardens. The statement has not been focused on the prospect, who has many hectares to cope with. The opening must relate the product to the prospect.

My service to companies with large grounds, and extensive gardens, is about the best you can get. According to the local press; and, my customers.

This is the best so far. It can be spoken with a suitable pause after the word 'get', and stress laid on 'according to the local press'; the final 'and my customers' is added as an afterthought. The appropriate press cutting will be available, of course.

If this opening works and stimulates discussion, it can be modified and used with private householders:

My service to residents with large gardens is about the best you can get. According to the local press; and, my customers.

A drawback with opening statements is that they do not always invite response. A question opening involves the prospect, but is often trickier to handle, especially if you fail to practise it.

If you open the sale with a question, consider all possible responses so that you can cope with them and continue the presentation. Here are some opening questions on the same theme:

Do you maintain your grounds and gardens with your own staff?

Are you able to maintain your grounds and gardens yourself?

Have you seen the local press comment on my gardening service?

If you needed a complete garden maintenance service, where could you obtain this?

Do you use an outside contractor for the maintenance of your grounds?

You certainly won't close every sale, but *every sale has to be opened*. It's worth practising openings because you have to do it every time you meet a possible client.

Establishing the need

Once you have opened the sale, it should be progressed to discover the prospect's real needs. You cannot ask, 'What do you really need?'; you have to determine this. The customer may not know his or her real need, in which case you should expand the conversation. You have to identify the need and make sure that the customer understands it.

Consider a man who visits his doctor for the required inoculations prior to a tropical visit. He doesn't want them and the two days of suffering they usually cause, but he *needs* them. While your product is unlikely to cause similar suffering to the customer, you must find out the need and make sure that the customer understands it.

You can appreciate the importance of having previously carried out an analysis of your product to determine the customer benefits. Keep these in mind as you progress the sales presentation with two kinds of questions: a closed question and an open probe.

Using closed questions

A closed question can be answered in one or two words:

Which colour do you prefer, the red or the blue?

I can do this on Wednesday; will that be all right?

Do you want just the one, or will you take a box?

Does it open to the left, or the right?

Is it more than ten metres?

Closed questions are used to narrow the conversation, move the presentation along a little more quickly, elicit specific information, or to get the prospect to make a decision.

Using open probes

An open probe is the opposite of a closed question. It cannot easily be answered by one or two words, but expands the conversation. It is used to obtain further information or opinion from the prospect:

Why is that?
How do you do it normally?
Really?
Could you explain that?
And, what happens after that?

Open and closed questions are used in the sales presentation according to whether you wish to open up the conversation, perhaps in search of needs, or to move it towards the close.

Coming to a resolution

Once the need has been established, and the customer is aware of it, he or she must resolve to satisfy that need. This is the main part of your sales presentation, but do not attempt to sell your product or service during this resolution stage. Explore the customer's problems, and make sure that he or she understands what is really needed and how this need can be satisfied – obviously keeping your product in mind.

Making the offer

When the customer knows what is needed and is resolved to satisfy it, then, and only then, should you make the offer. It is pointless making an offer before the need has been established, because the customer sees no reason to consider your suggestion.

Even when the need has been revealed, the customer still has to reach the resolution stage. This is where objections can arise, because the prospective customer may realize the need but may not wish to, or be unable to, resolve to satisfy it.

Making the offer too early – that is, before the need has been identified – will result in a 'No' decision.

Assessment

Remembering that good selling is really good buying, you should help the customer to assess the offer you have made. Have financial justifications available to back up your proposition. If the customer will save money by using your product or service, have evidence to support this. When you know sufficient about competitive products, and are experienced enough to venture in this direction, show how those products offer similar good value, but compare the advantages of your product, and how the buyer will be getting better value by buying yours.

Decision

When you consider that your offer has been adequately assessed and the buyer is ready to make a decision, close the sale – that is, ask for the order or whatever is your objective.

It may not be necessary to use all your sales presentation, your supporting points, references and financial justifications: the customer may be ready to buy at any time. Observe the buyer closely. When you see that he or she is prepared to buy, stop selling. The train has arrived at the station. Go for the close.

If that point has not been reached, don't let a 'No' stop you entirely: carry on with the presentation. It's similar to heating a piece of iron to change its shape: there is a point when it is hot enough but not before. You test, and if it's not ready, you put it back in the fire. A question framed in terms such as 'Is there any point that prevents your making a decision now?' will probably focus the conversation on any barrier.

A prospective buyer who travels from opening to close without seeing any barriers to buying will think that there must be something that has been overlooked, because it all seems too easy. The very fact that a barrier or objection has not arisen is often the very reason why the close is not made!

Selling

There will be times when it is unnecessary to go through the full sequence after opening the sale. When you and your products are known, and you know the customer, there is little point in exploring a customer's needs: you should know these! Occasionally you'll find on opening the sale that the customer goes straight to the decision and gives you an order.

Telephone selling

Whether you use the telephone to follow-up a sales lead, qualify a prospect, sell your product, or get an appointment with a possible customer, it is a technique that has to be learned and continually developed. Because the telephone can penetrate the innermost sanctum of a customer, you must be competent rather than clever, sympathetic and not sycophantic.

Pre-prepare your notepad with the name, address and phone number of the person you are calling. Have full information on your product or service with prices. Have a diary open at the appropriate week. If you are right-handed, hold the phone in your left hand, and have a pen ready.

Two golden rules: find out if it is convenient to talk with the person; say why you are phoning. But not:

Mr Jones? Is it convenient to talk with you? I want to tell you about my service.

Although this opening has obeyed the two rules, the prospect has had no time to reply. The following is better:

Good morning. Is that Mr Jones?

Yes. Who's that?

My name's Saunders. David Saunders. Mr Jones – is it convenient to talk with you at the moment?

Yes. Who did you say you were?

Saunders, Mr Jones. David Saunders. I have a small injection moulding shop and understand that your company buys plastics mouldings.

We do.

May I come and see you?

The conversation could go in any direction from here. If the prospect is interested in finding out there and then the extent of Saunders' injection-moulding capabilities, he will ask questions.

If Saunders' objective is to see Jones, he has to work to that end. The conversation might continue:

I'm rather busy at the moment. Can't you put details in the post?

This often happens.

Certainly. No problem sir. I said we were a small moulding shop but we have several hundred different mouldings. Are you interested in any particular type? For example, we have made a speciality of difficult re-entrant mouldings. Do you ever use these?

Saunders is using part of the *ONROAD* formula. He has opened the sale and is searching for the customer's need before making the offer.

When using the phone to make appointments with company directors, executives, managers, buyers and others, you will inevitably have to talk first with two guardians: the telephone operator and the personal secretary. Don't flannel; ask for help. Tell the receptionist that you would like to get an appointment with whoever, and could you talk with the secretary. When you are put through, remember that secretaries don't normally make decisions. They are employed to be secretaries, not to assess the merits of proposals that their bosses are paid to do. A truthful and sincere approach similar to the following, usually enlists their help:

I have a plastics moulding shop in the area and would like to see Mr Dungate to tell him about our products. It isn't something I can put in the post to him because there are so many variables. You see, as well as run-of-the-mill mouldings, we also specialize in difficult shapes and special plastics used by companies such as yours. Could you find me about twenty minutes one day next week please?

When you have prepared an opening statement such as this, practise saying it aloud. Some words or constructions may be difficult to say with ease: remove words that are not absolutely necessary. In the above example, the words 'used by companies such as yours' could be cut out to improve the flow. When ready, the opening should roll off the tongue without sounding glib.

Secretaries get to know a lot about the work of their boss, and often make decisions to prevent unwanted callers from being put through or having appointments. Make it clear that you have a proposition that their boss would want to know about.

Employing sales people

Consider the cost of employing a sales person. Basic salary, social security payments, holiday pay, sick pay, pension arrangements, sales commission or bonus, supervision: the overall cost can be daunting for the small firm. But if you are to expand, you will eventually need to employ sales people.

While the operation of a particular business would need to be evaluated in detail before deciding whether it could afford to employ someone, a quick calculation is as follows. Calculate the percentage profit earned on sales, and compare it with the cost of sales staff.

A small retailer with a yearly turnover of £50,000 and a profit of £14,000 – 28 per cent – is thinking of employing a sales person at a cost of £5,600 a year. This would effectively reduce profit to £8,400. Looked at in a different way, the cost of the sales person represents a turnover of $(5,600/28) \times 100 = £20,000$. As the retailer has been increasing business substantially over the previous two years he is confident that the extra person will enable him to devote more time to increasing sales.

Here is another illustration, concerning a silver-plating business in Somerset. Their rate of growth has averaged 12 per cent a year for the past seven years; their profit is 18 per cent. They estimated in December 1988 that to engage a full-time sales person, supply transport, pay for all the travelling expenses, would cost them about £20,000 a year. To break even on the annual cost of the sales person, they would need an increase in sales turnover of $(20,000/18) \times 100 = £111,100$. Even if they could have engaged someone at half the cost – £10,000 – they would need to increase sales by $(10,000/18) \times 100 = £55,000$. While their current turnover was nearly £200,000 a year, they decided that they could not afford to employ a full-time sales person.

Sales agents

A company that cannot afford to hire full-time sales people should consider appointing sales agents. A sales agent usually works on commission only, although in some circumstances he or she may be paid a nominal amount of expenses. Whether you use agents or full-time sales people, there are a number of factors of varying importance to be considered: these are shown in exhibit 8.1.

	Sales agent	Full-time sales person
Type of product and its application	Important	Very important
Servicing required by customers	Very important	Very important
Frequency of purchase	Can be important	Of interest
Calls per year on each customer	Relatively important	Very important
Time needed to open a new account	Not important	Very important
Time needed at each sales call	Not important	Important
Number of potential customers	Unimportant	Important
Density of customers	Of interest	Important
Size of territory	Of some interest	Important
Strength of competition	Of interest	Important
Transport provided	Not applicable	May be important

Exhibit 8.1 Sales territory factors

The reason why many of these factors are not important for a sales agent is that you do not pay for unproductive time. It is only when the agent achieves a sale that payment is made for services in the form of commission. This can be as high as a third of the selling price.

The first three factors shown in exhibit 8.1 are of particular interest when appointing agents.

Type of product and its application

Sales agents must like the product and feel comfortable selling it. If they have experience in selling a similar product, or know the market, so much the better.

Servicing required by customers

If customers need to be serviced, the sales agent must be reimbursed for the time spent servicing. This must be equal to the average commission that can be earned from a sale otherwise your customers will not receive adequate servicing. If the service element is substantial, separate service staff should be used. A good sales person should not be used to carry out routine jobs.

Frequency of purchase

This will vary from a single purchase to a high-repeat pattern. With products that are purchased only once, new customers have to be found continually. For products that are purchased frequently, sales people have to make repeat visits. While this should maintain sales, it restricts the area a sales person can cope with. Obviously, this is important when appointing full-time people, but may have some influence on the number of agents you appoint.

The density of potential customers and frequency of purchase will influence the size of territory, but you should appoint as many agents as you can and allocate territories based on their home town rather than nominating extensive territories. It is only natural that an agent will want as large a territory as possible: this is fine as long as sufficient sales roll in.

The sales mix

The different quantities of products bought by customers is your sales mix. You cannot dictate what they buy; you can influence their purchases by your pricing and advertising, but not control them. You may not be making the same profit on every product, and the product that is most popular is usually the one on which you receive least profit.

Exhibits 8.2 and 8.3 show two successive years' sales analysis of domestic tiles of a small retailer of home decoration products. They have five main types of tiles, type A is the most popular; it is also the least profitable. The profit on tiles in the first year was 11 per cent

Product	Sales	Sales mix	Profit (£)	(%)	Percentage of total profit
A	£10,500	53%	£840	8%	37%
B	£4,250	21%	£425	10%	19%
C	£2,400	12%	£360	15%	16%
D	£1,850	9%	£370	20%	17%
E	£1,000	5%	£250	25%	11%
Total	£20,000	100%	£2,245	11%	100%

Exhibit 8.2 Company sales mix

Product	Sales	Sales mix	Profit (£)	(%)	Percentage of total profit
A	£15,550	71%	£1,244	8%	57%
B	£3,000	14%	£300	10%	14%
C	£1,700	8%	£255	15%	12%
D	£1,000	4%	£200	20%	9%
E	£750	3%	£188	25%	8%
Total	£22,000	100%	£2,187	10%	100%

Exhibit 8.3 Changed sales mix

on sales of £20,000. Sales increased in the second year by 10 per cent to £22,000, but, because the sales mix changed, their profit fell.

While the sales mix cannot be controlled, it can be influenced by promoting those products that provide higher profit. In the third year the retailer greatly increased promotion for the two groups of the more profitable tiles (D and E), had prominent displays in the shop, and stressed their greater benefits to prospective customers. The results can be seen in exhibit 8.4. Sales of tiles increased by 25 per cent, from £22,000 to £27,600; profit increased by over 40 per cent, from £2,187 to £3,090.

Product	Sales	Sales mix	Profit (£)	(%)	Percentage of total profit
A	£17,500	63%	£1,400	8%	46%
B	£3,500	13%	£350	10%	11%
C	£1,850	7%	£277	15%	9%
D	£2,500	9%	£500	20%	16%
E	£2,250	8%	£563	25%	18%
Total	£27,600	100%	£3,090	11%	100%

Exhibit 8.4 Improved sales mix

Stock control

If you are marketing products, as your business expands it is normal that your stock expands, because holding stock provides a good distribution service to customers. If you cannot supply a customer because you are out of stock, the customer will try somewhere else. That is an order lost. Therefore you need to keep your stocks as high as possible.

However, stock represents money tied up: the greater your stock, the greater the expense. You have the cost of the stock and the cost of storing it. Therefore you need to keep your stocks as low as possible!

You have to compromise: your stocks must be adequate to give customers service equal to that of your competitors, but not too high to affect your cash and profit.

The best way to monitor stock levels is visually. If it is appropriate and possible, store your stock in convenient units so that you can see what you have. Enter your work-place every day through the stock room: you can see the situation immediately.

Stock has an effect on profits, but a greater, more immediate effect on cash: the more stock, the less cash you have. The amount of stock you carry must be related to the *order cycle time* (OCT). This is the time from placing an order to receiving the product.

If you are retailing consumer products, especially convenience goods, the OCT is very low. Most retailers have a weekly or twice-weekly replenishment of stock; for perishable goods it is daily. Customers expect to have a convenience good when they visit your shop, but for some products, such as furniture, the OCT can be many weeks.

If you are manufacturing products, the OCT must be comparable with those of your competitors. Some companies have built their reputation on their ability to supply customers faster than competitors, because speed of delivery often determines whether a sale is made.

The record industry falls into this category. With the massive demand for whatever pop record is in favour, stock has to be with the retail outlet within a maximum of forty-eight hours or the sale is lost. A computer printout of sales is generated twice a day for the record-pressing factory; production is geared to sales.

What is important in stock control is not the amount of stock but the *reliability* of stock. This is the number of orders or number of products that can be delivered within, say, twenty-four hours, whichever is appropriate.

For manufactured products, the manufacturing time must be taken into consideration when determining stock levels.

If you consider the sales of the tile retailer mentioned earlier, you can appreciate that his stock of tiles should be maintained relative to the volume break-down of the sales mix. The guidelines for keeping adequate stocks are:

- Stock mix must be related to volume sales mix.
- The quantity held should be just enough to supply everyone from stock, so that, as the last one is taken from stock, a new delivery is received.
- New stock is ordered when stock falls to a level that is sufficient to supply everyone until the new stock arrives.

These three guidelines assume an average rate of sale and that delivery time is constant. This situation is shown diagrammatically in exhibit 8.5: stock falls to zero as the new delivery arrives. If sales are irregular or delivery periods are variable, a minimum stock should be held: this situation is illustrated in exhibit 8.6.

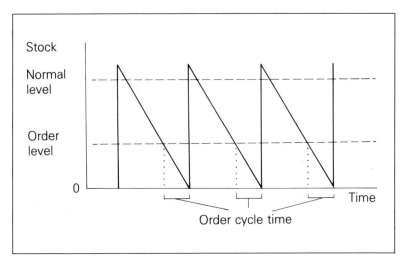

Exhibit 8.5 Stock levels

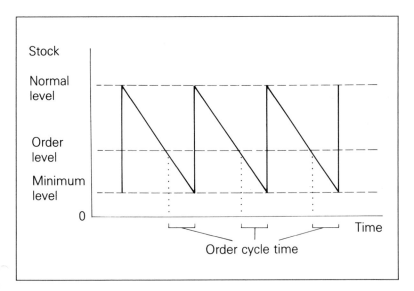

Exhibit 8.6 Stock levels with minimum stock

Commission as promotion

Commission is a sum of money that is a percentage of the net sales figure. It is paid to anyone at the discretion of the supplier of the product or service. If sales agents are used to obtain sales, they are normally paid commission on sales. The percentage commission varies according to the difficulty of selling the product: need products will have a much lower commission than want or desire products.

Three factors have to be considered:

- how performance is measured and payment calculated;
- percentage commission;
- the level at which payment starts.

Performance may be assessed on volume or value; the nature of the product or service will influence this. If a sales agent is used to sell John Gardner's gardening service, then performance is measured on the value of fees he obtains. For selling turbo shower-heads, value or volume might be used.

Value of sales is the more usual base. Profit should not be used as a base for paying commission, because the agent has no control over costs and expenses set against sales: it is bound to be a source of conflict.

The commission rate can be a percentage of turnover, different percentages of sales for different types of product, or a regular payment for each unit of sale. Commission may be paid immediately sales are made or after a quota of sales has been achieved.

In general, the difference between commission arrangements for full-time staff and commission-only agents concerns the percentage rate and when commission starts. Thus a full-time sales person might receive salary, expenses and a small incentive commission on all sales above an agreed level; the agent might receive a straight 25 per cent commission on all sales.

The case for a small business using commission-only agents has been suggested because of the cost angle. Other factors that might influence their use are:

- It is the usual practice in the particular industry.
- Adequate supervision of sales people is not possible.
- Considerable incentives are needed to sell the product.

When determining the comission rate, consider the profitability of the product, the difficulty of selling it, likely sales turnover and future potential, types of potential customers and where they are to be found.

The commission scheme should be simple to understand and simple to calculate. If the sales mix is likely to vary, or the profitability of products varies considerably, the commission rate may be different for each product or group of products.

A sliding scale could be used, with the commission rate increasing with turnover. This rate could either apply to all previous sales in the year, or only to sales above the appropriate levels of turnover.

A most important consideration is the time at which commission is paid. It could be paid when the order is received, when the goods are delivered, or when payment for them is received. If you pay commission immediately the order has been received, this will reduce your cash until the customer pays you. From the agent's viewpoint, the work has been done; time, energy and cost has been expended; the product has been sold; so commission should be paid.

You must estimate what sales you expect an agent to achieve, and the time taken by customers to settle their accounts, to arrive at the cash figure involved. A sale made near the end of a month will normally appear on the next month's statement. If the customer is given the usual thirty days to pay, you will be waiting for at least a couple of months for your money. You should calculate whether you can carry this sum for up to, say, four months, because customers are often slow in paying their bills. The better your sales agent, the more money you will need to budget for!

If you only pay commission when payment has been received from the customer, while this eases the cash situation, it is no incentive for the agent.

A compromise is to allow the agent a drawing account, enabling cash to be drawn up to a predetermined level related to the commission earned and moneys received. Again, from the agent's viewpoint, if money earned from sales is not paid promptly, a slightly higher commission would be justified.

Whatever system you adopt, calculate all possible sales figures and commissions payable to see the effect of your scheme. When you are satisfied, have the commission terms clearly set out, with examples to explain if necessary, and make sure that the agent understands them and agrees to them. These terms should be included in the letter of appointment, which should also contain a clause stating that should the agent cease to work for the company for any reason, commission ceases to be payable from that date. Finally, have your friendly solicitor look it over.

Sales management

Sales management is not so much the management of sales as the managing of sales people. Practically all sales managers have experience of selling, but it is not selling skills that are needed for successful sales management. The sales person promoted from the field to the position of sales manager, even if is at area or regional level, has to change from getting sales him- or herself to getting sales through the efforts of others. The essence of sales management might be summed up as the obtaining of sales through organizing, controlling and motivating the selling efforts of the sales team.

The sales team can be organized on a geographical basis or by products. The usual and more widely used scheme is a geographical basis, with each sales person allocated a specific territory that can be easily identified.

The product basis means specializing in a product or range of products, and covering the whole country. Although this can result in more than one sales person calling on the same company, as they would be selling different products, different buyers and technical people would be involved. For highly specialized products, it is preferable to organize the sales force on a product basis.

Control of the sales force should be based on the understanding that obtaining sales is a partnership – a partnership between the manager and the sales people. If an order that is confidently expected from a customer is in fact given to a competitor, the fault does not necessarily lie with the person in the field; it must be shared between the sales person and head office.

Selling is a lonely job, and sales people are highly sensitive to disappointment and encouragement. If they are left alone to do their job, they will gradually lack a sense of belonging. It is better that each sales person files a detailed weekly schedule of calls and a summary of intended calls for the following week. If contact is maintained with each person at least once a week, by phone, letter to home or hotel, or personal visit, the people in the field will know they belong to a company. Do it with care to avoid creating the impression that 'Big Brother is watching you'. The benefits that accrue from constant contact with the sales staff more than outweigh any disadvantages. Use the following six guidelines as a basis for managing sales personnel:

- Sales staff are aware of company procedure for planning and controlling progress from 'prospecting' to order.
- Sales staff meet on a regular basis to co-ordinate company approach to prospects.
- Sales staff know prospects' organizations, decision-makers, recommenders and the influencers.
- Sales staff set objectives for each meeting with a prospect.
- Sales staff regularly report on the number of prospects developed, number of early aborts, number of developed, number of conversions, miles per call, per order and cost per order.
- Sales staff receive regular training on activities that lead to major sales.

Key points

- Qualify all prospects by telephone before visiting them. When you have developed your technique, train someone else to do it.
- Develop a structured sales presentation that can be adopted by anyone who sells for you.
- Practise all openings and vital points in your presentation so that they communicate with the prospective customer.
- Before you can make an offer to a customer you must identify the real needs.
- Both stock and sales agents need to be well controlled.

9
Service

Outline

Service has two meanings: it describes the product, when it is a service such as consultancy, design, dry-cleaning, garden mainte-nance, hairdressing etc.; and it is also the assistance provided to make the handling of a product profitable for middlemen, and help the user of the product to get maximum satisfaction. This chapter is concerned with the second meaning: the assist-ance that a small business can render to users of its product or service and, to a lesser extent, the middlemen who may handle it. We look at:

- types of service
- the burden of before-sales and during-sales service
- the importance of after-sales-service
- service is part of the product
- the cost and obligations of service
- the 'cost of ownership' concept

Types of service

One thing a small business can excel at is the assistance it can give to users of its product or service, and to any middlemen who handle it – in a word, *service*. It includes all the help and advice afforded before an order is received: the support provided to people selling, and the servicing of the product after the sale has been made.

Before-sales service

Many products require a degree of service before the order is received. Quotations cannot simply be conjured up out of the blue: they may need measurements, extensive statistical and financial calculations, selection of materials, supply of samples from which a choice is made, and a discussion at the prospect's location.

A training company, invited to quote for the training of a company's employees, will need to visit the company, explore the training needs of the staff, suggest various training structures, consider these in detail, cost the operation, and submit a proposal for the prospect to consider.

John Gardner, asked to prepare a layout for a large domestic garden, will need to inspect the site, note the current layout, gradients and soil, and consider the client's ideas and wishes before submitting his suggestions.

The small engineering company that developed the turbo shower-head described in chapter 3 had to hand-machine samples of the product at a cost of about £14 each, arrange for independent tests, and send one to every company that expressed an interest.

All these are examples of before-sales service, which is not paid for, although, if an order is received, the profit should cover some of the work already done. If you provide a before-sales service that is too good, your fame will spread, and you may find a lot of people asking you for unpaid advice. This is particularly true of such things as advertising, kitchen designs, training recommendations, garden layouts etc.

The cost of all pre-sales service has to be recovered in the prices and fees charged generally, but you should avoid giving specific free advice – that is, particular advice for a client that should really be paid for. Give general advice and examples of suggestions provided to other clients, but don't prepare detailed layouts, recommendations and other expert guidance without payment.

If you quote or tender for work, or the nature of your product requires some service before a sale can be made, monitor the amount you provide, and keep it in proportion to the number of orders obtained.

Quotations and proposals

A *quotation* is a formal estimate to supply a specified product or service, detailing price or fee, delivery and payment terms. It is not a selling document but a formal offer to supply.

A *proposal* is a selling tool, containing the same information as a quotation but prepared in a such a way that it provides reasons why the customer should buy from you. A proposal should contain four essential sections:

- the prospect's need;
- your recommendation;
- the justification for buying from you;
- the warranty, guarantee and service provided.

To state the customer's need or objective, you must establish what the customer wishes to achieve by the acquisition of your product or service. If the product is being purchased for more than one purpose, those purposes should be listed – the most important first.

Recommendations must be linked with the customer's reasons for buying, showing how each of the needs will be met by the recommendation.

The justification for buying what you recommend should appear in the first sentence or two of this section. If the recommendation involves complex equipment and procedures, summarize them in this section and key them to a detailed appendix. The financial justification should be calculated on a modest and not ambitious level of operation. For example, if your product will 'pay for itself within six months', also show the projections for a year and eighteen months.

State your guarantee clearly: what you are prepared to vouch for and put right or replace free of charge, and over what period. Exhibit 9.1 is a proposal by John Gardner for the layout of a large domestic garden.

During-sales service

The service you provide when a sale is in progress is an adequate sales kit and training to do the job. Naturally, this service has to be organized in advance of the actual sales presentation. As you are unlikely to be using sales people until your business is well established,

Dear Mr Green

Following our meeting last week, when you approved the outline plan for the layout of the garden at Vine Cottage, Newton-on-Severn, I am now able to quote for this work. You require it to be laid out so that it will:

(a) Require minimum labour for upkeep.

(b) Have the walled-border flower-beds at height of 2 ft.

(c) Provide the garden with all-year-round interest, with attractive shrubs, foliage and flowers where possible.

(d) Make a feature of the pond on the east boundary.

(e) Allow for access of ride-on machinery for grass cutting, etc.

I recommend:

1. The garden is prepared according to the enclosed detailed plan on which the various features are indicated.

2. The border walls to have six courses of dressed Cotswold stone as illustrated in the enclosed photograph.

3. Locations of new plantings as marked on the plan, keyed to the appended list of trees, shrubs and flowers.

4. The pond is backed by a rockery of local granite and have a water pump for a constant flow of water over the stones.

5. Paths for access with machinery as marked on the plan enabling convenient storage in the barn.

6. We commence work before end of September so that all plantings, which are mainly in containers, will be well established before winter sets in.

While working on the pond, and connecting the electricity supply for the water pump, it would also be possible to install low-wattage underwater lighting. I have appended a separate quotation for the light; the extra labour is minimal and will involve no additional fee.

This layout is similar in extent to many I have carried out in the area and, as you will appreciate, my knowledge of local soil and climatic conditions is a major factor in making a success of such a venture.

All work is guaranteed to be to your entire satisfaction and, should any of the new plantings fail to become established within a year, we will replace them at no cost to you.

> Total price for all work, including the supply of all plants, shrubs, trees, Cotswold stone, water-pump:
>
> £2,250 (two thousand two hundred and fifty pounds) plus VAT.
>
> If you require the under-water light, this is an extra £28.75 (VAT inc.).
>
> Yours sincerely

Exhibit 9.1 A proposal

you will be doing your own selling and will have a first-hand experience of what is required.

The first requisite is product knowledge. If you are selling a manufactured product, this data must include information on the materials, components and methods used in its manufacture, its versatility and limitations, its uses. A comparative analysis, similar to exhibits 3.2, 3.3 and 3.4, should be used to position it and to provide the basis for the sales presentation.

If the product can be handled during the sales presentation, this must be practised. Nothing destroys confidence in a product quicker than the sales person trying to find how to open it, switch it on, or fumbling with the demonstration, and being unsure of its operation.

A businessman with a franchise in Devon and Cornwall for a domestic appliance is skilled in demonstrating it to guest house owners who are his prospective customers. He recounts that all went well until the first time he was asked if it was robust, and if it would stand up to handling by visitors. He placed the appliance on the floor, stood on it and jumped up and down a little. Unfortunately, he stood on the plastic crest fixed to the metal case. The crest fractured and shattered into many little pieces over the floor. While the case was more than adequate to withstand his gymnastic demonstration, the plastic emblem was not. With nimble presence of mind, he said, 'I'm always doing that!' and, showing the appliance to the prospect, added, 'As you can see, the case is very robust. I have another badge in the car. It's easy to fix.' He made the sale!

You should develop your own sales presentation along the lines discussed in chapter 8, and, if appropriate, have a sales presenter prepared. This can be as simple as a series of well-displayed, easy-to-read facts, photographs and illustrations in plastic envelopes, or various sales aids, up to a portable video display unit with a cassette ready to show to the prospect.

As your business expands, you should develop the sales presenter into a sales manual. The sales manual is also a training aid, and contains full data on products and sales procedures that your future sales agents and employees should know. If you start thinking about the sales manual from the time you commence business, it will be less of a burden when you need to compile it and hand it to your first sales person. A manual should contain, as a minimum:

- the background of the business, its owners, products and policies;
- a description of the position of a sales agent, sales person, duties and responsibilities;
- a description of the sales organization and field supervision;
- a general description of the market, customers and prospective customers;
- a specimen sales presentation and full instructions on product handling or variations of services offered;
- a procedure for dealing with complaints;
- advice on the management of sales territory and seeking customers;
- a summary of routine, non-selling tasks such as administration and procedure for sales expenses etc.

If you distribute your products through middlemen, a large part of your success will depend on the back-up and service you give them. A good profit margin is a major consideration, but informative sales literature, sales aids, in-store demonstrations, dealer staff training, and anything that makes it easy for them to sell will yield dividends.

After-sales service

A product is purchased for what it will do, not for what it is. Therefore the assistance you provide to users should be directed to maintaining their satisfaction with the product. A secondary objective is that their satisfaction will be relayed to their friends and acquaintances; and a future objective is that when the time comes for a replacement to be purchased, your product will be chosen.

Obviously, some products need no after-sales service; for others the type of product will dictate the degree of after-sales service necessary.

There are four main categories of after-sales service:

- educational;
- installation;
- maintenance;
- repair.

Probably the most important is educational servicing, because the user often has to interpret printed instructions on the use of the product. If these are not readily grasped, a certain animosity develops against the product. Technical products and complex consumer products need to be studied before they can be used, but even in this hi-tech age the number of people each year who require hospital treatment because they are bitten by the common deck-chair is almost unbelievable.

You may be selling a product with instructions supplied. If you think that they are open to misinterpretation, amplify them for your customers. If the product or service is your own, and you have to prepare your own instructions, you should, if appropriate, key the text to the illustrations. When the draft is finished, try it out on someone of ordinary intelligence.

Installation and routine maintenance are usually for industrial machines, equipment, or domestic apparatus. Delivery and installation in the UK is a service normally included in the price of the product. If you venture into the European 'single market', delivery is arranged at the time of purchase but installation is organized separately, often by a different department, and charged for.

Repairs should not worry you unduly in the early days, but you must plan for contingencies: you might be required to repair a product shortly after you start operations. The type and size of product will dictate whether repair and maintenance can be carried out in the user's premises, or it can be returned to a service depot. If your business continues to expand, and you decide to use locally appointed service engineers, you will need to support them with:

- product training;
- training in maintenance and repair techniques;
- an adequate stock of spares and replacements.

It is sound business practice to train all service engineers in the art of selling replacement products. When an existing product is no longer worth repairing, the service engineer is best placed to be the sales person.

Complaints

An important area of after-sales service is dealing with complaints. These shouldn't happen very often, but when they do, the way they are handled should be a good advertisement for your business. A complaint should be treated as an emergency: it needs immediate attention at a level where it can be put right.

Install a complaints procedure and make everyone in your business aware of it. This does not mean having a suitable form to be completed; it means that you have a swift procedure to placate the customer and remove the cause of the complaint as quickly as possible.

It is not unknown for customers to make unjustifiable complaints, so your procedure must acknowledge the complaint but not admit that the company is at fault. By the way you deal with a complaint, you can turn it into a benefit. A difficulty sometimes arises where a customer makes a complaint in good faith but is mistaken.

The author received a complaint from a woman diner in his restaurant that the trout she had ordered was not cooked properly; she said that it was not cooked in the middle, and still raw. There followed an apology, and the removal of the offending trout to the kitchen. There, the salmon-trout was found to be perfectly cooked: what the woman thought was 'raw' was the natural colour of the fish. What does one do in such circumstances? Take it back and tell her that there's nothing wrong with it? Say, 'You stupid woman; have you never had salmon-trout before?'

The customer has to be allowed to save face. The author returned, told the customer that the chef would cook her another one, and asked if she would accept a complimentary half bottle of dry white wine to keep her company while she was waiting. As the wine was being poured, she was asked if she wanted salmon-trout or would she prefer a rainbow trout. She didn't mind which. Another trout was served shortly afterwards, and the incident was closed.

The value of dealing with a complaint in this way is the subsequent publicity it is bound to create. That story of the trout will be told to friends, colleagues and acquaintances, and, sooner or later, the woman will learn that salmon-trout tends to stay pink after cooking. The value of the advertising was many times the cost of the trout.

When the opportunity presents itself, try to turn a complaint into an advantage.

Service is part of the product

Products are purchased because they satisfy some specific need. Service must ensure that the product will measure up to the expectations of the purchaser. Major products, such as large printing machinery, are operated by the supplier, with the buyers' employees being trained during this running-in period. The machinery is only handed over once it is operating properly and the buyers' staff is able to handle it.

A service that is often part of a computer software program is the right to purchase any future updated version at a special price.

Even the small distributor of domestic garden equipment will often ensure when delivering it that the new owner is able to handle it, and get maximum benefit from its use. Such small distributors don't stay small very long, because they include this service as part of the product.

If this initial service is provided as a matter of course when the product is sold, it should be *free*, its cost being recovered in the price of the product.

Cost and obligations of service

Costs of servicing will average out over time and enable you to produce a list of service charges. However, early in a product's life-cycle, especially with complex or technical products, servicing costs are higher than the long-term average, and must be allowed for in the price structure.

A major obligation of the manufacturer of a product that will eventually need replacement and repairs is the obligation to carry adequate stock of parts to service the product for its normal life – say, ten years.

With many new hi-tech products, the stability and likely longevity of an organization are critical considerations for an intending buyer. Success is possible if new companies in such a field are able to show that their backing is substantial enough, and that they will be in existence in five years' time.

The cost-of-ownership concept

When professional buyers are considering the acquisition of plant, equipment and machinery, in addition to quality, delivery, and service, they are interested in two aspects of the price: the initial cost and the operating cost. Apart from the cost of any consumable items used by the product, different products have different degrees of operating efficiency. Some use less energy or are more economical in use of materials; some work for longer periods between routine maintenance or require less servicing. This servicing element is frequently a major factor in the purchasing decision.

From the start, products wear, and eventually components need replacing. A product will only perform at high efficiency if it is regularly serviced. Professional buyers consider this aspect very carefully when selecting products. It is not just the cost of a product that matters, but the initial cost plus the cost of servicing: this is the cost of ownership.

Consumers are not so aware of this concept. In fact, for many consumer capital goods, the ready availability of extended credit and hire purchase agreements means that it is often the initial down-payment that decides what is purchased.

Whatever type of product you are marketing, you should include information relating to its operating costs and servicing costs.

Key points

- While the small business can excel in the service it provides to customers, don't allow unpaid pre-sales service to get out of hand.
- When quoting for business make your quotation into a selling document by submitting a proposal.
- If you are selling a product, or a service that makes use of a product, practise handling it so that you are thoroughly skilled in its use before you demonstrate it to the potential customer.
- The way you handle complaints can change a dissatisfied customer into a loyal one. Treat all complaints as you would a person with a heart attack – have an emergency procedure to put into action immediately.
- No one buys a product for itself alone but for what it will do. Service helps to keep the product sold.

10

Planning

Outline

A small business is close to its market, is flexible, can operate on slim margins, and implement decisions rapidly. It usually has limited resources, not enough staff, and often works under conditions less than adequate: in a word, it is vulnerable. A marketing plan to guide your decisions and actions is desirable. We look at:

- developing the marketing plan
- constructing a sales forecast and budget
- planning the advertising
- the selling plan
- controlling the plan
- cash budgeting

The marketing plan

Planning your business must begin before you start the business. It must be possible to sell enough of your products or service to make reasonable profits. A *marketing plan* is a statement of intentions to achieve desired results, and some indication of how it is proposed to attain them.

The basis of your planning must be accurate data; it need not be detailed at this stage, but it must be accurate. You probably have some idea of where you intend to start your business and the size and type of premises needed. Before you commit yourself to buy or rent, thoroughly inspect the location. Make sure that it is convenient for you, and for your customers and suppliers. See if there are adequate car parking facilities nearby, that power and lighting supplies are sufficient, that telephone service is readily available, that water and drainage are adequate. Check for any local restrictions in force or planned: for one-way streets, pedestrian precincts, delivery of goods, low bridges, limited-weight bridges, and also local amenities and public transport.

If location is important for the catchment area, spend several days visiting the local shops, cafés and any hotels, to judge the type of customers that frequent the area. Visit the local services – library, banks, council offices and other traders – and ask questions.

Location may not be important as long as you have adequate ware-housing and transportation facilities. Gather data on your product and its competitors, on the market and any trends. If you are making your product, what quantity can you make? How much will it cost to make? How long will it take, and how many people are involved? Compared with competition, how much can you sell it for? Can you make sufficient profit?

Collect all this information in a file, and make a note of any important points on paper: don't rely on your memory.

Although you will have a mass of information, your marketing plan should be clear, and as simple as possible. In general, it has five main sections:

- the products and their servicing;
- the customers who will form the market and/or sub-markets;
- the price structure and discounts;
- the sales and promotional methods to be used;
- an estimate of the results to be obtained within a given period of time.

When you are employing people, you will need to expand your ideas into a formal plan. This involves deciding what are the *key tasks*, agreeing *objectives* in terms of results to be achieved within certain time scales, and setting acceptable *performance levels*. All these should be linked with control, measuring performance against objectives, interpreting trends and results, and taking any necessary corrective action at the right time.

For the small business, especially one just starting up, the five sections are a guide to what you have to think about: product, customer, price, promotion, and estimates of sales, expenses and profits.

A franchise

If you are thinking of acquiring a franchise, a lot of this basic planning will be done by the franchisor. But, although the franchisor has a interest in your continuing success, it will be *your* business, so you must carry out your own appraisal.

The product or service should be reasonably well-known to the people who comprise its market, and there should be a strong possibility that there will be a demand for the product in the foreseeable future.

A fashion product is unlikely to be an attractive venture for the first-time small business person. If appropriate, the franchisor should have a programme of research and development. To test this, find out what major innovations have been introduced in recent years.

Some companies are reasonably well known in the market but have only recently started franchising their product or service, and it may not have been proven. The number of franchises that have been taken up in the previous three years will indicate the attractiveness of the venture. You should have a discussion with two or three of these, and find out the average time it took to get their business up and running, and into a profitable situation.

Inspect copies of the franchisor's accounts for the previous few years and seek your bank manager's opinion. You will need to pay the franchisor an initial lump sum, but this should be modest – between 2 and 10 per cent of the total setting-up cost. It should not be a major source of revenue for the franchisor, who should be more interested in a percentage of your future profits.

More detailed advice can be obtained from the Franchise Association – the address is at the back of this guide.

If you decide that there is little that a franchisor can do for you that you cannot do yourself, this chapter is much more important.

Key tasks

Commit the key tasks of your plan in writing. If it will help, have them displayed on the wall in front of where you work so that you can see them every day. They form your main business aims.

Concentrate on them. A service company in Reading, started by one man in 1986 and now employing four other people, still has its original marketing plan on the wall in front of the owner's workspace; it is shown in exhibit 10.1. Only the delivery period has changed; '48 hours' has been crossed through and '3 days' written in.

KEY TASKS

Market my service throughout the county of Berkshire.

Promote the service with classified ads and direct mail.

Sell direct to users – householders – with personal calls.

Sell at one price level but discount for long-term contracts.

Hold a stock of accessories to ensure 48-hour delivery.

Sell mainly cash-on-completion, only give credit where essential.

Keep the level of debtors below 3 per cent of sales.

Exhibit 10.1 Key tasks of a marketing plan

As you expand and employ staff, your marketing plan will need to be more detailed. Exhibit 10.2 is the first page of the marketing plan for a small company in Kent, with a turnover of well under £1 million. (The name of the product has been changed to preserve its anonymity.)

Sales forecast

With the key tasks of your plan settled, you should construct a *sales forecast* – an estimate of what you think your sales will be for the first year. Estimating sales is always a mixture of calculation and conjecture.

If you are selling a product, consider how long it will take to sell the first one, then the next, and the next; consider how many you

---

MARKETING PLAN KEY TASKS

To market the existing, new and improved FACIL products nationally throughout the UK, to laboratories and scientific departments of universities and large companies.

To provide a full customer service for dimensional variations from standard FACIL products to:
    (a)   Increase company control over the specials market.
    (b)   Remove the onus of special order problems from stockists.

To promote national interest in FACIL products and stimulate orders being placed through stockists.

To test market new products regionally before being launched nationally.

To develop sales of new products with OEMs, government departments and large organizations where it is considered that local stockists cannot profitably handle the extra work involved.

To maintain current business in standard FACIL products through stockists and not divert it, explicitly or implicitly, to the company.

To preserve present good relations with stockists and require all sales staff to maintain regular contacts.

To reduce finished goods stock from 5 per cent to 4 per cent of turnover in one year.

To reduce the debtors figure from 4 per cent to 3 per cent of turnover in one year.

Exhibit 10.2 Key marketing tasks of larger company

might sell in the first three months, and so on until you have a *guesstimate* for the year.

If you are supplying a service, consider how long it takes to undertake the service and when you might reasonably expect to obtain your first, second and third orders. In a similar manner to constructing a sales forecast of products, make a conservative estimate of sales turnover for the year.

Break down this sales forecast into convenient periods, say, months, allowing for seasonal variations. If you expect your sales to be higher

in summer or in winter, increase the estimates for the appropriate
months, and decrease the others: the total should remain the same
of course. Exhibit 10.3 is a break-down of a total sales estimate for
one hundred, with sales expected to be higher in the summer
months. Allowance has been made for a gradual start, only nine
sales for the first three months, compared with nineteen for the last
three. Sales are forecast to be above average from May to September,
with the bulk of the sales – 42 per cent – in the three summer
months.

	Jan	Feb	Mar	Apl	May	Jun	Jul	Aug	Sep	Oct	Nov	Dec
Sales	1	3	5	8	12	15	15	12	10	10	6	3

Sales estimate for the year 19X1

Exhibit 10.3 Seasonally adjusted sales estimate

Sales budget

The *sales budget* is the sales forecast with all the costs and expenses
to achieve it calculated and included. Whichever is appropriate,
calculate the costs of materials and labour to produce your forecast
turnover, and all the expenses of the business, rent, rates etc., as
listed in exhibit 10.4, a form you can copy and use.

Planning the advertising attack

Decide on a sum of money for publicity that you think is sufficient
to accomplish your marketing plan. Many different formulae exist
to determine the advertising appropriation. At the end of the year,
accountants, auditors and the tax people all calculate the total spent
on advertising as a percentage of sales. Seldom over a year should it
rise above 5 per cent. Therefore assume that you will only achieve
about 75 per cent of your sales estimate, and keep the allocation for

SALES BUDGET FOR 19X1

	Budget (£)	Actual (£)	Budget (£)	Actual (£)
Sales . . . . . . @ £			. . . . . .	. . . . . .
Materials	. . . . . .	. . . . . .		
Direct labour	. . . . . .	. . . . . .		
Total direct costs:			. . . . . .	. . . . . .
Gross profit			. . . . . .	. . . . . .
Rent	. . . . . .	. . . . . .		
Rates	. . . . . .	. . . . . .		
Water rates	. . . . . .	. . . . . .		
Insurance	. . . . . .	. . . . . .		
Heat, light, power	. . . . . .	. . . . . .		
Repairs & maintenance	. . . . . .	. . . . . .		
Motor car	. . . . . .	. . . . . .		
Travelling	. . . . . .	. . . . . .		
Advertising	. . . . . .	. . . . . .		
Postage	. . . . . .	. . . . . .		
Packaging	. . . . . .	. . . . . .		
Delivery	. . . . . .	. . . . . .		
Stationery	. . . . . .	. . . . . .		
Telephone	. . . . . .	. . . . . .		
Wages	. . . . . .	. . . . . .		
Cleaning	. . . . . .	. . . . . .		
Consumable items	. . . . . .	. . . . . .		
Personal drawings	. . . . . .	. . . . . .		
Professional fees	. . . . . .	. . . . . .		
Interest on loans	. . . . . .	. . . . . .		
Bank charges	. . . . . .	. . . . . .		
Repayment of loan	. . . . . .	. . . . . .		
Total			. . . . . .	. . . . . .
Net profit before tax			. . . . . .	. . . . . .

Exhibit 10.4 Profit and loss budget

advertising below 5 per cent of that figure. If you estimate your sales will be £20,000 in the first year, allocate 5 per cent of 75 per cent of this figure – £750.

Because you have allocated an amount, it doesn't mean that you have to spend it. On the other hand, it has to be sufficient to publicize your business in the first year. Customers will be unaware of you, and you have to surmount this initial ignorance with enough publicity. As you will have seen in chapter 6, a sustained programme of publicity is necessary, especially during the first year or so, until you are established.

Because sales fail to develop as you planned, don't make the mistake of blaming the advertising. Gauge what the advertising has to achieve, and base your plan on sound reasoning.

Relate the advertising plan to the marketing plan for the *type* of messages to be publicized; relate it to the sales forecast for the *task* to be accomplished.

Consider the tasks in exhibit 10.1 – selling direct to householder users in the county of Berkshire. How many households does the sales forecast indicate have to purchase? Assume that a sale will be made to one in twenty who respond in some way to the advertising. How many households have to see, or receive, the message? Say only 1 per cent of the total who could see it, actually do see it. How many have to be appealed to?

Basing the argument on these suppositions, and an estimate to sell to fifty households during the year, this means that $50 \times 20 = 1,000$ are needed to respond to the advertising. If this represents the 1 per cent who will notice the message, the advertising has to be projected to 100,000 households.

The Office of Population, Censuses and Surveys records a population of 134,000 in Reading alone. With an average of, say, 2.5 people per household, this is over 50,000 households. Therefore it would be prudent to concentrate on the city of Reading and expand to the rest of the county as turnover increases.

The *Reading Evening Post*, which circulates in Berkshire, has a circulation of about 30,000. Distribution data of the newspaper can be obtained from the publishers, and will indicate the percentages of sales within successively larger areas of the centre. However, if the estimated statistics are valid, it is not possible to reach 100,000 households using only this paper.

At this point in planning, it is advisable to review projections to see if undue pessimism or optimism has been introduced into the assumed figures. Exhibit 10.5, with various response percentages, estimates the different numbers of prospects to be tackled to obtain sales of fifty.

[1]	[2]	[3]	[4]
	To obtain	Percentage	Need to
	50 sales	of readers	project ads to
Ratio of respondents	[1] × 50	who could see ad	100/[3] × [2]
to each sale			
10	500	1%	50,000
10	500	2%	25,000
10	500	5%	10,000
20	1,000	1%	100,000
20	1,000	2%	50,000
20	1,000	5%	20,000
30	1,500	1%	150,000
30	1,500	2%	75,000
30	1,500	5%	30,000
40	2,000	1%	200,000
40	2,000	2%	100,000
40	2,000	5%	40,000
50	2,500	1%	250,000
50	2,500	2%	125,000
50	2,500	5%	50,000

Exhibit 10.5 Conjecturing advertising reach

The percentage of readers who will notice the advertisement (column [3]) could be increased by using larger advertisements, but for the small business person this is hardly practicable. The size and frequency of the adverts must be within the capacity of the business: this is a constraint you must observe.

Even if you achieved an extremely high noting of your advertisement in the newspaper, it is still restricted by the paper's circulation and readership total. You would need supporting advertising, and this could best be done with direct mail.

However, despite these considerations, obtaining a response is a means to an end; getting the order is the goal. In exhibit 6.10, which we looked at in chapter 6, the emphasis is on the number of responses to a mailing. While this measurement is significant for mailings or advertisements at the first stage of your plan, the second stage – conversion of enquiries to orders – is more important.

Clearly, substantial effort has to be directed to the ratio of *sales* to respondents – the conversion factor. At one in twenty it's 5 per cent;

at one in fifty, 2 per cent. A reasonable marketing objective would be to aim for a 10 per cent conversion factor by enthusiastic follow-up letters and a persuasive sales presentation.

The selling plan

Common to all selling situations, whether you have to visit potential customers or they visit you, is the process shown in exhibit 10.6.

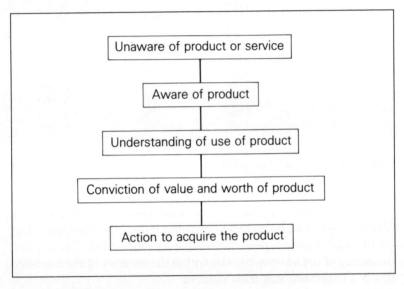

Exhibit 10.6 The selling process

At first, target customers are unaware of the existence of your product. Changing ignorance of your product into awareness is comparatively easy; straightforward announcements by word of mouth, by sales people, signs, window display, adverts, or editorial mentions in newspapers can make people aware of your product. Not all people, but some; perhaps some of your target market.

Developing awareness into an understanding of your product and its use requires further descriptive or educational inputs. These may be delivered by advertising, but the selling activity is usually required – if not to deliver them, to reinforce them.

The next steps are large ones, and the core of the selling process. It is changing people's understanding of the product's use, to being convinced of its value and worth, and, once convinced, taking the final step: the decision to buy.

If you are now marketing-oriented, you will appreciate that this process should not be directed so much to selling your product, as to *buying your product*.

If customers have to visit you, your initial task is to publicize your existence. If your premises are in the High Street, suitable signs and a window display will advertise your presence. If you are in a back street, regular local newspaper advertising with a simple map showing your location is necessary. This should be supported with a reprint of the ad, which can be used for sales literature. Don't simply circulate these on a door-to-door basis: target potential customers.

For example, if you are offering a service to, say, car drivers, arrange for your sales leaflets to be inserted under the windscreen-wipers of parked cars. You may need to dress up the literature in colour to gain attention, because uninvited leaflets placed under windscreen-wipers often engender hostility.

If you have to visit potential customers, plan your calls. This is best organized on a geographic basis: calling on a maximum number in one area to reduce travelling time. If you are working on your own, plan to call two or three days a week depending on the time you have to spend at base.

If your product requires little consideration to make the buying decision, you could call without an appointment – cold canvassing. However, you would be introducing a large element of chance in your selling activity. You may not see anyone, or the person you do see may not be the right one.

Few products are purchased without some measure of deliberation: to sell them, appointments must be made. These can best be arranged by phone as discussed in chapter 8.

Prepare customer contact records grouped in areas, and develop a format for recording company, address, phone number, name and position of contacts, secretary's name, and best time to call. Exhibit 10.7 is a specimen contact record.

```
┌─────────────────────────────────────────────────────────────┐
│                  CUSTOMER CONTACT RECORD                      │
│                                                               │
│   Customer _____     Ref. no. _____      │
│   Address  _____     Phone _____      │
│            _____     Best time _____      │
│            _____     Date started ____     │
│                                                               │
│                                               Date (S)een     │
│       Key People*          Position           or (P)honed     │
│                                                               │
│   _____    _____       _____      │
│   _____    _____       _____      │
│                        (Secretary)                            │
│   _____    _____       _____      │
│   _____    _____       _____      │
│   _____    _____       _____      │
│                                                               │
│   *Indicate (D)ecision maker, (R)ecommender, or (I)influencer │
│                                                               │
│   Approx. order value £ _____   Demo dates _____      │
│   Product details (continue on reverse):                      │
│                                                               │
│                                                               │
│   Who, what are we up against? (Continue on reverse)          │
│                                                               │
│                                                               │
│                                                               │
│   Action to be taken or follow up, with date:                 │
│                                                               │
└─────────────────────────────────────────────────────────────┘
```

Exhibit 10.7 Specimen customer record sheet

Planning and control

When making a marketing decision, remember that basically it is finding customers who have need of your product (they may not know it), and then satisfying that need by selling it to them. But *every marketing decision is a money decision*. It is this fundamental fact, which is misunderstood, often ignored, or is even unknown, that causes so many major problems in companies, especially in the small business.

A marketing decision costs money; it should never be made

without being evaluated for the initial and likely future cost, and the period of time before a return is expected. A large company can afford to make mistakes, even a few big mistakes; a small business that makes a big mistake often finds itself in difficulties.

From the outset resolve to make all your marketing plans and decisions in the light of their financial implications. Produce too much or too little and you will run into rough financial waters; sell too much or too little and you will also have financial difficulties.

Planning and control of any plan must be considered together: they are not separate, unconnected activities. While you are working alone, you prepare the plan and control its implementation. When you employ other people, you should delegate parts of it to them, but remember that the plan will only be as good as the people who control it.

Bits of paper, note pads, printed forms, a Filofax – all have their uses, but prepare tables as recommended in this guide and use a calculator for all figures. It is imperative to control all quantitative aspects of your business so that you know what is happening, and can quickly determine the current position at any time.

If you have use of a personal computer and a spreadsheet program, you will save hours of time. However, unless you have guidance and the formulae to insert, setting it up will take you ages. The control procedures that follow can all be done with paper, pencil and calculator, but are much quicker and less prone to accidental errors if you have a computer.

Cash flow

Cash is necessary to keep the business running, therefore control of cash flow is essential. It's no use waiting until you have run out of cash before you take action; you must have a control system that monitors the position monthly, weekly, or daily, depending on the nature of your business. You decide the levels at which action must be taken, and include these in the control procedure.

With your sales forecast prepared, as in exhibit 10.3, and sales budget, along the lines of exhibit 10.4, you can project an estimated *cash flow budget*. This is a statement of the inward and outward cash flows, expected and actual, for a period. Exhibit 10.8 shows an example for a six-month period of sales relating to the forecast in exhibit 10.3. Raw data are inserted and the relationships and cash flows calculated:

- Actual sales and actual costs are inserted each month.
- Budgeted costs (costs and expenses) are calculated at a constant 72 per cent of the sales forecast for each month. You can alter this percentage.
- Estimated cash flow is the sales estimate less the budgeted costs.

Actual cash flow for the month is compared with the budgeted cash flow; if it is similar to budget, no action is needed. *You have to decide what percentage of variation is acceptable.* In this table:

- 15 per cent below budget is signalled for action.
- If cash flow in any month is 25 per cent higher than budget, the situation is signalled for exploiting.

The overall cash position compares the cumulative total cash budgeted with the balance as at the end of each month.

- Variation of 10 per cent is allowed in the cash balance. If the cash balance falls below 90 per cent of the budgeted amount, action is indicated.

This table and others in the guide have been prepared on a personal computer using a standard spreadsheet package. All the relationships between the figures are predetermined, and changes are made automatically. If you want details of using the computer in the control of your business, see *The Barclays Guide to Computing for the Small Business.*

Expanded analysis

Keep your control procedures as simple as possible: there is no point in developing statistical analyses unless you use them. Exhibit 10.8 is perfectly adequate for the marketing of a service or product which is bought in.

If you manufacture a product, you must keep more detailed records. The analysis in exhibit 10.9 has been split into three sections, one for each of the six months, plus the profit and loss

			Estimated Cash Flow (£)			
	Jan	Feb	Mar	Apl	May	Jun
Sales estimate	125	375	625	1,000	1,250	1,500
Actual sales	125	250	500	1,300	780	1,400
Budgeted costs	90	270	450	720	900	1,080
Actual costs	80	300	425	800	1,000	1,100
Estimated cash flow	35	105	175	280	350	420
Actual cash flow	45	(50)	75	500	(220)	300
Cash balance	45	(5)	70	570	350	650
Action?	–none–	ACTION!	ACTION!	–none–	ACTION!	ACTION!
Exploit?	EXPLOIT	–no–	–no–	EXPLOIT	–no–	–no–
OVERALL POSITION	OK!	ACTION!	ACTION!	OK!	ACTION!	ACTION!

Exhibit 10.8 Cash budget for six months

account. It contains details of production and expenses, together with control percentages. These control percentages have been calculated for each month and *cumulative to each month*. Thus each month's efforts and the year to date can be assessed together. This is important because a particularly good or bad month may hide the overall position for the year to date. (The formulae for these and other tables will be found in *The Barclays Guide to Computing for the Small Business.*)

The occasional unit discrepancies in the analyses arise because the forms have been generated on a computer spreadsheet which was programmed to round up the figures to whole numbers.

Cost of materials is calculated at a constant 10 per cent of sales. The analysis allows for a normal thirty days settlement of accounts; thus a two-month delay is shown for receipts from sales. A small amount of part-time labour at £50 a month is paid.

Overheads are calculated at 5 per cent of the total of materials and labour. Salaries are the monthly drawings by the owner. Social security is 15 per cent of labour and salaries. Distribution is 4 per cent of sales. It is assumed that no interest is payable in January, and no balance of money is brought forward from December. Interest, at a nominal 1 per cent a month, is presumed to be payable from February.

In exhibit 10.9 a net profit of £2,418 is shown for the year, but there is a negative cash balance every month, and at the end of the year £332 is owed. Payments for November and December sales still

	Estimated Cash Flow (£s)					
	Jan	Feb	Mar	Apl	May	Jun
Sales	300	400	500	750	1,000	1,500
Cumulative turnover	300	700	1,200	1,950	2,950	4,450
Revenue			300	400	500	750
Cash out						
Purchase of assets						
Materials	30	40	50	75	100	150
Labour	50	50	50	50	50	50
Overheads	4	5	5	6	8	10
Total product cost	84	95	105	131	158	210
Salaries	500	500	500	500	500	500
Social security	83	83	83	83	83	83
Distribution	12	16	20	30	40	60
Insurance			17			17
Phone, postage	20	20	20	20	20	20
Advertising	25	25	25	25	25	25
Total expenses	640	644	664	658	668	704
Total cash out	724	738	769	789	825	914
Cash flow	(724)	(738)	(469)	(389)	(325)	(164)
Interest		(7)	(15)	(20)	(24)	(27)
Balance b/fwd		(724)	(1,469)	(1,952)	(2,361)	(2,709)
Balance c/fwd	(724)	(1,469)	(1,952)	(2,361)	(2,709)	(2,900)
Monthly analysis January to June						
Materials % of product	36%	42%	48%	57%	63%	71%
Labour % of product	60%	53%	48%	38%	32%	24%
Product % of sales	28%	24%	21%	18%	16%	14%
Salaries % of sales	167%	125%	100%	67%	50%	33%
Expenses % of sales	213%	161%	133%	88%	67%	47%
Advertising % of sales	8%	6%	5%	3%	3%	2%
Cumulative analysis January to June						
Materials % of product	36%	39%	42%	47%	52%	57%
Labour % of product	60%	56%	53%	48%	44%	38%
Product % of sales	28%	26%	24%	21%	19%	18%
Salaries % of sales	167%	143%	125%	103%	85%	67%
Expenses % of sales	213%	183%	162%	134%	111%	89%
Advertising % of sales	8%	7%	6%	5%	4%	3%

Exhibit 10.9(a) Expanded analysis for January to June
Note: Unit discrepancies in some columns are the result of integers rounded up on computer.

	Estimated Cash Flow (£s)					
	Jul	Aug	Sep	Oct	Nov	Dec
Sales	1,250	1,250	1,500	1,500	1,500	1,250
Cumulative turnover	5,700	6,950	8,450	9,950	11,450	12,700
Revenue	1,000	1,500	1,250	1,250	1,500	1,500
Cash out						
Purchase of assets						
Materials	125	125	150	150	150	125
Labour	50	50	50	50	50	50
Overheads	9	9	10	10	10	9
Total product cost	184	184	210	210	210	184
Salaries	500	500	500	500	500	500
Social security	83	83	83	83	83	83
Distribution	50	50	60	60	60	50
Insurance			17			17
Phone, postage	20	20	20	20	20	20
Advertising	25	25	25	25	25	25
Total expenses	678	678	704	688	688	694
Total cash out	861	861	914	898	898	878
Cash flow	139	639	336	353	603	622
Interest	(29)	(28)	(22)	(19)	(15)	(9)
Balance b/fwd	(2,900)	(2,791)	(2,180)	(1,866)	(1,532)	(945)
Balance c/fwd	(2,791)	(2,180)	(1,866)	(1,532)	(945)	(332)
Monthly analysis July to December						
Materials % of product	68%	68%	71%	71%	71%	68%
Labour % of product	27%	27%	24%	24%	24%	27%
Product % of sales	15%	15%	14%	14%	14%	15%
Salaries % of sales	40%	40%	33%	33%	33%	40%
Expenses % of sales	54%	54%	47%	46%	46%	56%
Advertising % of sales	2%	2%	2%	2%	2%	2%
Cumulative analysis July to December						
Materials % of product	59%	60%	62%	63%	64%	65%
Labour % of product	36%	35%	33%	32%	31%	31%
Product % of sales	17%	17%	16%	16%	16%	15%
Salaries % of sales	61%	58%	53%	50%	48%	47%
Expenses % of sales	82%	77%	71%	68%	65%	64%
Advertising % of sales	3%	3%	3%	3%	2%	2%

Exhibit 10.9(b) Expanded analysis for July to December

Note: Unit discrepancies in some columns are the result of integers rounded up on computer.

	£	£
Turnover		12,700
Production		
Materials	1,270	
Labour	600	
Overheads	94	
		1,964
Gross profit		10,737
Less expenses		
Salaries	6,000	
Social security	990	
Distribution	508	
Insurance	66	
Phone & post	240	
Advertising	300	
Interest	214	
		8,318
Net profit		£2,418

Exhibit 10.9(c) Profit and loss account

have to be received, £1,500+£1,250 = £2,750; this, less the £332 negative balance, is the net profit of £2,418.

The monthly and cumulative analyses are used to control the business. Performance for each month is assessed and compared with the performance of the year to date. In a start-up situation it is natural for expenses of running the business – salaries, wages, advertising etc. – to be high in the early months. But these should gradually level out to an acceptable percentage. This is what you have to watch for.

If the owner's drawing of £500 a month is partly for producing the product, then the analysis needs amending because the total production cost ignores this. Whatever portion of the £500 is reckoned to be for production should be transferred to the production row.

Materials are a high percentage of total production costs, and level out at around 68 per cent. This is an important figure to watch:

high material costs cannot always be avoided, whereas high labour costs indicate a danger area. The two should be compared continually. In this analysis the labour content is a little over 30 per cent for the year. These two percentages may be used as yardsticks for subsequent forecasts. Production cost, as a percentage of sales, is a healthy low figure at 15 per cent over the year, and draws our attention to the other costs.

Because sales start low and have a seasonal peak during summer, salaries and expenses need to be considered very carefully. Naturally they are high at the beginning, but are still running at a level of over 60 per cent by the end of the year.

Action must be taken to reduce these expenses, and serious consideration given to the drawings figure of £500 a month. Both are too high and will have a serious effect on the ability of the business to grow, especially if sales are less than forecast.

Failing to make quota

The above analysis has been edited from the initial projection of a small businessman who started his business in his garage in Slough. He had assumed 100 per cent sales, and had not considered what his position might be if he failed to make his quota of sales. Fortunately he took advice before launching his product, and made crucial amendments. In the event, by the end of twelve months, he achieved a commendable 80 per cent of his target and had a number of substantial sales pending. The failure to achieve his forecast by some 20 per cent had a marked effect on his position, but had been foreseen as a possibility.

Failing to achieve the level of sales estimated is the most common cause of small business problems.

In your planning you should calculate the position if less than 100 per cent is achieved – say, 80 per cent and 50 per cent levels. Exhibit 10.9 is modified. 'Sales' is changed to 'Estimated sales', and two rows inserted after this and also after 'Estimated sales' for the second six months. These two new rows for each six-month section are labelled 'Percentage performance' and 'Actual sales'. This new layout is illustrated in exhibit 10.10.

		Estimated Cash Flow (£s)				
	Jan	Feb	Mar	Apl	May	Jun
Estimated sales	300	400	500	750	1,000	1,500
Percentage performance	80%	80%	80%	80%	80%	80%
Actual sales	240	320	400	600	800	1,200
Cumulative turnover	240	560	960	1,560	2,360	3,560
Revenue			240	320	400	600
Cash out						
Purchase of assets						
Materials	24	32	40	60	80	120
Labour	50	50	50	50	50	50
Overheads	4	4	5	6	7	9
Total product cost	78	86	95	116	137	179
Salaries	500	500	500	500	500	500
Social security	83	83	83	83	83	83
Distribution	10	13	16	24	32	48
Insurance			17			17
Phone, postage	20	20	20	20	20	20
Advertising	25	25	25	25	25	25
Total expenses	637	640	660	652	660	692
Total cash out	715	726	755	767	796	871
Cash flow	(715)	(726)	(515)	(447)	(396)	(271)
Interest		(7)	(14)	(20)	(24)	(29)
Balance b/fwd		(715)	(1,448)	(1,977)	(2,444)	(2,865)
Balance c/fwd	(715)	(1,448)	(1,977)	(2,444)	(2,865)	(3,164)

Monthly analysis January to June

	Jan	Feb	Mar	Apl	May	Jun
Materials % of product	31%	37%	42%	52%	59%	67%
Labour % of product	64%	58%	53%	43%	37%	28%
Product % of sales	32%	27%	24%	19%	17%	15%
Salaries % of sales	208%	156%	125%	83%	63%	42%
Expenses % of sales	265%	200%	165%	109%	82%	58%
Advertising % of sales	10%	8%	6%	4%	3%	2%

Cumulative analysis January to June

	Jan	Feb	Mar	Apl	May	Jun
Materials % of product	31%	34%	37%	42%	46%	52%
Labour % of product	64%	61%	58%	54%	49%	44%
Product % of sales	32%	29%	27%	24%	22%	19%
Salaries % of sales	208%	179%	156%	128%	106%	84%
Expenses % of sales	265%	228%	202%	166%	138%	111%
Advertising % of sales	10%	9%	8%	6%	5%	4%

Exhibit 10.10(a) Performance at 80 per cent for January to June
Note: Unit discrepancies in some columns are the result of integers rounded up on computer.

	Estimated Cash Flow (£s)					
	Jul	Aug	Sep	Oct	Nov	Dec
Estimated sales	1,250	1,250	1,500	1,500	1,500	1,250
Percentage performance	80%	80%	80%	80%	80%	80%
Actual sales	1,000	1,000	1,200	1,200	1,200	1,000
Cumulative turnover	4,560	5,560	6,760	7,960	9,160	10,160
Revenue	800	1,200	1,000	1,000	1,200	1,200
Cash out						
Purchase of assets						
Materials	100	100	120	120	120	100
Labour	50	50	50	50	50	50
Overheads	8	8	9	9	9	8
Total product cost	158	158	179	179	179	158
Salaries	500	500	500	500	500	500
Social security	83	83	83	83	83	83
Distribution	40	40	48	48	48	40
Insurance			17			17
Phone, postage	20	20	20	20	20	20
Advertising	25	25	25	25	25	25
Total expenses	668	668	692	676	676	684
Total cash out	825	825	871	854	854	842
Cash flow	(25)	375	130	146	346	359
Interest	(32)	(32)	(29)	(28)	(27)	(23)
Balance b/fwd	(3,164)	(3,220)	(2,878)	(2,777)	(2,659)	(2,339)
Balance c/fwd	(3,220)	(2,878)	(2,777)	(2,659)	(2,339)	(2,004)

Monthly analysis July to December

Materials % of product	63%	63%	67%	67%	67%	63%
Labour % of product	32%	32%	28%	28%	28%	32%
Product % of sales	16%	16%	15%	15%	15%	16%
Salaries % of sales	50%	50%	42%	42%	42%	50%
Expenses % of sales	67%	67%	58%	56%	56%	68%
Advertising % of sales	3%	3%	2%	2%	2%	3%

Cumulative analysis July to December

Materials % of product	54%	55%	57%	58%	60%	60%
Labour % of product	41%	40%	38%	37%	36%	35%
Product % of sales	19%	18%	17%	17%	17%	17%
Salaries % of sales	77%	72%	67%	63%	60%	59%
Expenses % of sales	101%	95%	88%	83%	80%	79%
Advertising % of sales	4%	4%	3%	3%	3%	3%

Exhibit 10.10(b) Performance at 80 per cent for July to December

Note: Unit discrepancies in some columns are the result of integers rounded up on computer.

	£	£
Turnover		10,160
Production		
Materials	1,016	
Labour	600	
Overheads	81	
		1,697
Gross profit		8,463
Less expenses		
Salaries	6,000	
Social security	990	
Distribution	406	
Insurance	66	
Phone & post	240	
Advertising	300	
Interest	265	
		8,267
Net profit		£196

Exhibit 10.10(c) Profit and loss account at 80 per cent performance

Decide what percentage performance you think is worth looking at – say, 80 per cent. Multiply the estimated monthly sales by this percentage performance figure. At 80 per cent performance net profit is down to £196, cash never goes positive during the year, and there is a final negative balance of £2,004. A borrowing level of over £3,200 is needed during the year.

The analyses are enlightening. At 80 per cent operation, costs relative to turnover soar. It's not before August that the cumulative expenses total falls to less than 100 per cent of the sales figure! They are far too high at around 80 per cent of sales for the year, and this is because the business was operating at 20 per cent below the level forecast.

Suppose sales have been seriously over-estimated and only 50 per cent performance is achieved. Exhibit 10.11 shows the result at 50 per cent performance. There is a loss of £3,137 and a negative balance

		Estimated Cash Flow (£s)				
	Jan	Feb	Mar	Apl	May	Jun
Estimated sales	300	400	500	750	1,000	1,500
Percentage performance	50%	50%	50%	50%	50%	50%
Actual sales	150	200	250	375	500	750
Cumulative turnover	150	350	600	975	1,475	2,225
Revenue			150	200	250	375
Cash out						
Purchase of assets						
Materials	15	20	25	38	50	75
Labour	50	50	50	50	50	50
Overheads	3	4	4	4	5	6
Total product cost	68	74	79	92	105	131
Salaries	500	500	500	500	500	500
Social security	83	83	83	83	83	83
Distribution	6	8	10	15	20	30
Insurance			17			17
Phone, postage	20	20	20	20	20	20
Advertising	25	25	25	25	25	25
Total expenses	634	636	654	643	648	674
Total cash out	702	709	733	734	753	805
Cash flow	(702)	(709)	(583)	(534)	(503)	(430)
Interest		(7)	(14)	(20)	(26)	(31)
Balance b/fwd		(702)	(1,418)	(2,015)	(2,569)	(3,097)
Balance c/fwd	(702)	(1,418)	(2,015)	(2,569)	(3,097)	(3,559)

Monthly analysis January to June						
Materials % of product	22%	27%	32%	41%	48%	57%
Labour % of product	73%	68%	63%	54%	48%	38%
Product % of sales	46%	37%	32%	25%	21%	18%
Salaries % of sales	333%	250%	200%	133%	100%	67%
Expenses % of sales	422%	318%	262%	171%	130%	90%
Advertising % of sales	17%	13%	10%	7%	5%	3%

Cumulative analysis January to June						
Materials % of product	22%	25%	27%	31%	35%	41%
Labour % of product	73%	71%	68%	64%	60%	55%
Product % of sales	46%	41%	37%	32%	28%	25%
Salaries % of sales	333%	286%	250%	205%	169%	135%
Expenses % of sales	422%	363%	321%	263%	218%	175%
Advertising % of sales	17%	14%	13%	10%	8%	7%

Exhibit 10.11(a) Analysis at 50 per cent performance for January to June
Note: Unit discrepancies in some columns are the result of integers rounded up on computer.

		Estimated Cash Flow (£s)				
	Jul	Aug	Sep	Oct	Nov	Dec
Estimated sales	1,250	1,250	1,500	1,500	1,500	1,250
Percentage performance	50%	50%	50%	50%	50%	50%
Actual sales	625	625	750	750	750	625
Cumulative turnover	2,850	3,475	4,225	4,975	5,725	6,350
Revenue	500	750	625	625	750	750
Cash out						
Purchase of assets						
Materials	63	63	75	75	75	63
Labour	50	50	50	50	50	50
Overheads	6	6	6	6	6	6
Total product cost	118	118	131	131	131	118
Salaries	500	500	500	500	500	500
Social security	83	83	83	83	83	83
Distribution	25	25	30	30	30	25
Insurance			17			17
Phone, postage	20	20	20	20	20	20
Advertising	25	25	25	25	25	25
Total expenses	653	653	674	658	658	669
Total cash out	771	771	805	789	789	787
Cash flow	(271)	(21)	(180)	(164)	(39)	(37)
Interest	(36)	(39)	(39)	(41)	(43)	(44)
Balance b/fwd	(3,559)	(3,865)	(3,924)	(4,144)	(4,349)	(4,431)
Balance c/fwd	(3,865)	(3,924)	(4,144)	(4,349)	(4,431)	(4,512)

Monthly analysis July to December

Materials % of product	53%	53%	57%	57%	57%	53%
Labour % of product	42%	42%	38%	38%	38%	42%
Product % of sales	19%	19%	18%	18%	18%	19%
Salaries % of sales	80%	80%	67%	67%	67%	80%
Expenses % of sales	104%	104%	90%	88%	88%	107%
Advertising % of sales	4%	4%	3%	3%	3%	4%

Cumulative analysis July to December

Materials % of product	43%	44%	46%	47%	49%	49%
Labour % of product	52%	51%	49%	48%	47%	46%
Product % of sales	23%	23%	22%	21%	21%	20%
Salaries % of sales	123%	115%	107%	101%	96%	94%
Expenses % of sales	159%	149%	139%	131%	125%	124%
Advertising % of sales	6%	6%	5%	5%	5%	5%

Exhibit 10.11(b) Analysis at 50 per cent performance for July to December
Note: Unit discrepancies in some columns are the result of integers rounded up on computer.

	£	£
Turnover		6,350
Production		
Materials	635	
Labour	600	
Overheads	62	
		1,297
Gross profit		5,053
Less expenses		
Salaries	6,000	
Social security	990	
Distribution	254	
Insurance	66	
Phone & post	240	
Advertising	300	
Interest	341	
		8,191
Net profit		£(3,137)

Exhibit 10.11(c) Profit and loss projection at 50 per cent performance

at the end of the year of £4,512. The borrowing increases dramatically during the year with over £4,500 needed to keep going.

Again it is the absurdly high expenses figure which is continually more than the sales figure. This leads to an important conclusion in planning. *Expenses should always total less than the most pessimistic sales figure.*

Environmental adaptation

Business enterprises adapt to their environment. This acculturation is an intrinsic quality of the type of business. Some companies have to be big to survive: iron, steel, glass-making, generation of electricity, aeroplane manufacture. This size factor confronts European computer manufacturers in the 1990s: more will have to merge to survive.

In contrast, most small businesses stay small because an optimum level of operation has been achieved. They have four general stages: fight for life, struggle for survival, battle for growth, fulfilment. The appetite for a fight decreases as the owner of the business approaches contentment. Over 80 per cent of all British enterprises have a turnover of under £250,000. Many theories have been advanced: the entrepreneurial trap, fear of losing control, family compromise. The truth is more likely to be that their owners prefer it that way: they have become happy engine-drivers.

Key points

- Use your marketing plan to guide the content and treatment of your advertising plan; relate the advertising plan to the sales forecast for the task that has to be accomplished.
- Everything in the sales and marketing plan should be concentrated on the task of getting orders.
- Aim your advertising at an area that you can satisfactorily service yourself or with limited staff.
- Project your sales estimate for a year and decide the percentage level of under-performance at which you need to take action.
- Prepare a cash flow forecast and highlight the control points that need to be examined every month, week or day.

Appendix: Sources of information

Organizations

Advisory, Conciliation and Arbitration Service (ACAS)
Clifton House
83–117 Euston Road
London
NW1 2RB

Offers guidance and assistance on a wide range of employment issues. A series of free advisory books is available.

Alliance of Small Firms and Self-Employed People Ltd
33 The Green
Calne
Wilts
SN11 8DJ

Aims to represent the interests of members at national and local level. Membership fee £25 a year. Provides a newsletter and advice on a wide range of business matters and offers a consultancy service.

Association of British Directory Publishers
17 Kingsway
London
WC2B 6UN

The Association's member companies (nearly 50) publish directories to a high professional standard. Members range from small, highly specialized publishers to large international organizations issuing hundreds of directories a year.

Association of Independent Businesses
Trowbray House
108 Weston Street
London
SE1 3QB

Aims to promote the interests of the smaller business and maintains contact with government departments and parliament. Can advise on useful sources of advice for the small business person.

Association of International Courier and Express Services (AICES)
PO Box 10
Leatherhead
Surrey
KT22 0HY

The Association's members are air couriers who undertake collection, international transportation and delivery of time-sensitive business documents and small packages from the UK to any address overseas.

BAR (Agents Register) Ltd
24 Mount Parade
Harrogate
HG1 1BP

Of value when you are looking for a sales agent. Membership is £35. Advertisements may be placed in the monthly review.

British Direct Marketing Association
Grosvenor Gardens House
Grosvenor Gardens
London
SW1W 0BS

An association of three main groups: direct mail companies who will supply lists and services to users; organizations who market direct to users and not through retailers and stockists; consultancies and agencies that specialize in direct marketing methods.

British Export Houses Association
16 Dartmouth Street
London
SW1H 9BL

An association of export intermediaries who tend to specialize in particular markets or products, and function in several capacities such as merchants, manufacturers' agents, export managers, buying or confirming houses, export finance houses etc.

British Franchise Association
Franchise Chambers
Thames View
Newtown Road
Henley-on-Thames
Oxon
RD9 1HG

Formed in 1977 by a number of companies engaged in marketing goods and services through independent outlets. The Association's aims include the establishing of standards to assist members of the public, press, potential investors and government bodies in differentiating between sound business opportunities and suspect offers. A Franchisee Information Pack, and a Franchisor's Manual are available at a nominal cost.

British Institute of Management
Management House
Parker Street
London
WC2B 5PT

Offers comprehensive services to members.

British List Brokers Association
Springfield House
Princess Street
Bedminster
Bristol
BS3 4EF

An association of companies who will supply lists for direct mail.

British Market Research Bureau Ltd
Saunders House
53 The Mall
London
W5 3TE

Undertakes research, mostly for large companies.

British Overseas Trade Board
Department of Trade And Industry
1 Victoria Street
London
SW1H 0ET

Provides information and assistance for companies wishing to export.

British Standards Institution
2 Park Street
London
W1A 2BS

Provides advice on standards in the UK and other countries.

Business Statistics Office
Cardiff Road
Newport
Gwent
NP9 1XG

A central agency that collects data on manufacturing industries.

Central Office of Information
Hercules Road
London
SE1 7DU

Provides a wide range of services, some of which are particularly useful to the exporter.

Commission for Racial Equality
Elliot House
10/12 Allington Street
London
SW1E 5EH

Has a code of practice which explains how to avoid discrimination in employment.

Companies Registration Office
Companies House
Crown Way
Maindy
Cardiff
CF4 3UZ

Responsible for the registration of companies and enquiries under the Companies Act.

Confederation of British Industry
Centre Point
103 New Oxford Street
London
WC1A 1DU

Provides a wide range of services for small businesses who are members.

Cooperative Development Agency
Broadmead House
21 Panton Street
London
SW1Y 4DR

Established by Parliament to promote workers' co-operatives, of which there are now over 1,500, each employing an average of twenty people. Members of co-operatives must benefit primarily as workers and not solely as investors; members have equal control; interest payments to members are restricted to prevent unlimited distribution of funds; surpluses are retained in the co-operative or distributed to members according to their involvement. Membership is open to anyone satisfying the entry qualifications.

Croner Publications
Croner House
173 Kingston Road
New Malden
Surrey
KT3 3SS

Publishes material of interest to exporters.

Current British Directories
CBD Research Ltd
154 High Street
Beckenham
Kent
BR3 1EA

Able to advise on suitable directories covering every industry.

Data Protection Registrar
Springfield House
Water Lane
Wilmslow
Cheshire
SK9 5AX

Under the Data Protection Act, anyone keeping data on individuals on computer files must register. The registrar can provide an information pack.

Department of Health and Social Security
Alexander Fleming House
Elephant and Castle
London
SE1 6BY

Provides advice on what is necessary when you employ people part-time or full-time.

Department of Trade and Industry
Ashdown House
123 Victoria Street
London
SW1E 6RB

Supplies a vast amount of information and advice covering every aspect of trade and industry, home and overseas.

Design Council
28 Haymarket
London
SW1Y 4SU

Provides a free advisory design service to industry.

Direct Mail Producers Association
34 Grand Avenue
London
N10 3BP

Over 100 members offer consultancy, creative design, print management, mailings, lists, packaging etc. Of particular interest to the small business is the free advice available to companies wishing to use direct mail.

Direct Mail Sales Bureau
14 Floral Street
London
WC2E 9RR

Advises on direct mail activities.

Direct Mail Services Standards Board
26 Eccleston Street
London
SW1W 9PY

The Board's purpose is to maintain and enhance professional and ethical standards among the suppliers of direct mail services, and to confer recognition on suppliers who meet those standards. Will provide advice for advertisers in selecting from the recognized agencies offering services appropriate to the particular need.

Dun & Bradstreet Ltd
26–32 Clifton Street
London
EC2P 2LY

Supplies information, products and services relating to commercial credit and collections; advertising; direct mail; energy research and services; human-resource management; sales and sales management; strategic planning; television and media research; manufacturing, distribution, and processing; economic and financial analysis and investment planning; marketing, market research and product development; banking and insurance. Free booklets are available on their services.

Equal Opportunities Commission
Overseas House
Quay Street
Manchester
M3 3HN

Has a code of practice that explains how to avoid discrimination in recruitment. The law requires companies with twenty or more employees to employ registered disabled workers amounting to at least 3 per cent of the workforce or to obtain an exemption permit from a Disablement Resettlement Officer of the Manpower Services Commission.

Export Credit Guarantee Department
Export House
Ludgate Hill
London
EC4M 7AY

Arranges insurance cover for export payment risks.

Health and Safety Executive
St Hughes House
Stanley Precinct
Bootle
L20 3QY

Is concerned with securing compliance with health and safety legislation at work.

Institute of Export
64 Clifton Street
London
EC2A 4HB

Aims to provide a forum of exchange of experience and information between exporters. An education and training scheme covers the whole field of exporting. Issues a monthly journal.

Institute of Freight Forwarders Ltd
Suffield House
9 Paradise Road
Richmond
Surrey
TW9 1SA

Provides information on freight-forwarders who carry out the handling and through-transport arrangements for UK exports.

Institute of Marketing
Moor Hall
Cookham
Maidenhead
Berks
SL6 9QH

A chartered institute that offers advice, courses and publications on all aspects of marketing.

International Chamber of Commerce
Centre Point
103 New Oxford Street
London
WC1A 1QB

Publishes a range of booklets on documentation and payment for exported goods.

Kelly's Directories
Neville House
Eden Street
Kingston-upon-Thames
Surrey
KT1 1BY

Publishes a range of trade directories which may be viewed in the public library.

Kompass Publishers Ltd
RAC House
Lansdowne Road
Croydon
Surrey
CR9 2HH

Publishes a range of directories covering all trades and countries. The local library usually possesses copies.

Manufacturers' Agents Association (MAA)
Lonsdale House
7/11 High Street
Reigate
Surrey
RH2 9AA

If you want to become a self-employed agent, this association can advise you. Membership is £34.50 a year plus a joining fee.

National Federation of Self-Employed and Small Businesses Ltd
32 St Annes Road
West Lytham
St Annes
Lancashire
FY8 1NY

A substantial association of over 50,000 members in the UK with adequate funds to take test cases through the courts at every level. Membership is £24 a year. Provides a legal expenses compensation cover scheme, for VAT, Health and Safety Regulations, Inland Revenue investigations and industrial tribunals.

A. C. Nielsen Co. Ltd
Headington
Oxford

Has extensive marketing research facilities. Free booklets are available on their services which are normally for big companies.

Resource
1–3 Birdcage Walk
London
SW1H 9JH

An independent organization sponsored jointly by the Government and British Standards Institute. Promotes technical co-operation in key overseas markets for standards, quality assurance, metrology, testing, and their application to industrial and agricultural development and technology.

Royal Mail Direct Marketing Section
Post Office Headquarters
33 Grosvenor Place
London
SW1X 1PX

Provides free advice on direct mail activities, campaign planning, mailing lists, designing and writing, testing and analysis.

Rural Development Commission (RDC)
11 Cowley Street
London
SW1P 3NA

also

141 Castle Street
Salisbury
Wilts
SP1 3TP

Combines RDC and the Council for Small Industries in Rural Areas (CoSIRA). Provides advice and consultancy services to small businesses in rural areas.

Scottish Development Agency
Small Business Division
Rosebery House
Haymarket Terrace
Edinburgh
EH12 5EZ

Provides a free information and counselling service; publishes a range of booklets; and can advise on exporting, industrial relations, marketing, market research, training and Government aid. The Agency is the largest provider of industrial and commercial space in Scotland.

Sell's Publications Ltd
Sell's House
39 East Street
Epsom
Surrey
KT17 1BQ

Publishes the following directories: *Sell's Directory of Products and Services*; *Sell's Scottish Directory*; *Health Service Buyer's Guide*; *Marina Guide* (UK and Holland); *Aerospace Europe*; *Sell's Building Index*; *Government and Municipal Contractors*; *Hotel, Restaurant and Catering Supplies*; *Sell's British Exporters*; *Sell's Marine Market*.

Small Claims Court

The booklets *Small Claims in the County Court: How to Sue and Defend Actions without a Solicitor* and *Enforcing Money Judgments in the County Court: How to Obtain Payment without a Solicitor* are available from any County Court.

Small Firms Service

Has thirteen offices throughout the UK. Dial 100 and ask for Freefone Enterprise.

Standard Industrial Classification

HMSO
PO Box 569
London
SE1 9NH

Provides a classification for every conceivable type of industry.

Training Agency
Moorfoot
Sheffield

Government training organization that sponsors a number of Business Growth Training Options run at various places throughout the country. The Private Enterprise Programme currently offers thirteen different seminars, each one lasting a day.

Wages Inspectorate
Steel House
11 Tothill Street
London
SW1H 9NF

Of interest to companies employing people. An employee aged 21 and over in an industry covered by a wages council is entitled to be paid at least the statutory minimum rate that is contained in the Wages Council order. These rates are updated annually and enforced by the Inspectorate.

Welsh Development Agency
Small Business Unit
Treforest Industrial Estate
Pontypridd
Mid Glamorgan
CF37 5UT

Offers a comprehensive range of support for small businesses. Can help with finding premises, counselling, consultancy, obtaining advice and information. A comprehensive range of booklets and literature is available on every aspect to guide the small business. Currently there is a scheme where individuals can license plant, equipment and machinery to start manufacturing products before actually setting up in business on their own.

Books and publications

ANBAR Abstracts

These can be inspected at the local reference library. Abstracts of selected articles covering advertising, design, marketing planning, market research, new product development, purchasing, retailing, transportation, stock control.

Franchise World
James House
37 Nottingham Road
London
SW17 7EA

Magazine of franchise opportunities. Also publish a newsletter and the *Directory of Franchising*.

Marketing Pocket Book
NTC Publications Ltd
PO Box 69
Henley-on-Thames
Oxon
RG9 2BZ

If you have to buy only one book on marketing information, this is a must. Only 16cm×11cm, and 128 pages, but packed with vital information on: economic and demographic data; the consumer; distribution; advertising and promotional expenditure; media; and international data. Over 60 sources are used every year to update the book.

The Small Firms Service National Reference Book

Computerized database on 3.5″ or 5.25″ disks for the small business providing useful contacts, information on a subject, publications, reference sources, suggested reading etc. Over 100 subject headings.

Colin Barrow, *Small Business Guide* (BBC Publications)

Godfrey Golzen, Colin Barrow and Jackie Severn, *Taking up a Franchise* (Kogan Page)

Martin Mendlesohn, *How to Evaluate a Franchise* (Franchise Publications)

Len Rogers, *Handbook of Sales and Marketing Management* (Kogan Page)

218

Len Rogers, *Selling by Telephone* (Kogan Page)

See also the other books in the *Barclays Small Business Series*. An up-to-date list appears at the front of this volume.

Glossary

average stock A statistical estimate indicating the volume or value of products held in stock. The most crude is *opening* plus *closing stock* divided by two. A more accurate figure would be stock held 1 January plus the stock figures for the last day of each month, divided by thirteen.

brand image The customers' total impression of, and feeling for, a product or brand.

concentrated marketing Strategy that recognizes different characteristics of a total market and selects one segment to which to appeal.

convenience goods Products that are purchased when convenient to the buyer and which do not need a special shopping expedition.

cost-pricing Setting the price of the product or service near to its cost.

decision-making unit A formal or informal group of people in a company who, together, influence and decide which suppliers are suitable.

differential marketing A marketing strategy that distinguishes different parts or segments of the market and makes unique appeals to that segment.

direct mail Publicity with letters and other advertising material that make use of the postal system.

durables A class of consumer products that are substantial and long-lasting, therefore not frequently purchased.

elasticity of demand The sensitivity of changes in demand for a product according to small changes in price.

folder A publicity leaflet that is folded one or more times.

impulse goods Convenience goods that are bought on the spur of the moment.

leaflet A single sheet of printed paper used for publicity.

market A substantial number of people or companies with needs, the money or credit availability to satisfy those needs, and the willingness to satisfy them.

market coverage The percentage of the total market that suppliers are able to reach with their current distribution system.

market forecast An estimate of the total sales of a product likely to be made in a market by all competitors.

market penetration The degree to which a company has established active connections in a distribution channel. The term is also used of the percentage share of the total market.

market segment A part of the total market that can be distinguished by known characteristics such as geographical location, size, type of industry, etc.

market share Proportion of the possible market sales of a product or service consistently captured by a company.

marketing mix The product, price, place, promotion and service that are combined in different ways to appeal to different types of market.

marketing research Umbrella term often contracted to 'market research' which covers three activities: product research; distribution and advertising research; market research. Investigations and surveys to determine the acceptability of a product, how it is, or could be, distributed and publicized, and the characteristics of the customers who comprise the market.

mark-up Percentage applied to the cost of a product to arrive at a price. The percentage profit made on a sale is not the mark-up but the actual profit expressed as a percentage of the price. Thus a mark-up of 25 per cent results in a profit of 20 per cent; a mark-up of a third, results in a profit of 25 per cent.

media Various means by which messages about a product or service can be transmitted to potential customers. The five main media are: press; television; posters and other outdoor advertising; radio; cinema.

need, want, desire Terms to describe customers' requirements and yearnings for products and services. At the top of the list are the essentials or needs; lower down the list and towards the bottom are the non-essentials or desires.

non-durable goods A class of consumer products that are frequently purchased and do not normally last a long time

penetration pricing A low-price strategy to obtain as many sales as possible in as short a time as possible.

pre-emptive pricing A pricing strategy similar to penetration pricing but with the objective of preventing competitors from entering the market.

price bracket A price range in which a customer is prepared to buy a product.

price plateau   Same as price bracket.

product attribute   A characteristic or quality of a product.

product benefit   A product attribute that provides a specific satisfaction to customers.

product differentiation   Making a product different from competitive products in the eyes of customers. The difference may be real, intrinsic in the product, or only in the mind of the customer.

product positioning   Determining the combined image that people have, or would have, of a product; its standing and reputation compared with similar or alternative products. A product could therefore be developed to occupy a specific position in the market.

prospects   Those who were *suspects* and have been partly qualified as prospective or potential customers.

qualifying leads   The process of contacting *suspects* and *prospects* to determine if they are potential customers, whether they have a need of the product, appreciate its cost, have the necessary funds to acquire it, and when they may be ready to purchase it.

sales estimate   Same as sales forecast.

sales forecast   An estimate, in volume or value, of sales of a product for a given future period, using a specific marketing plan, and under an assumed set of economic circumstances.

sales mix   The sales of different products from a company's total range of products.

segmentation   Division of the total market into groups of potential customers possessing similar needs and characteristics, so that they can be treated as separate markets.

shopping goods   A class of products for which customers 'go shopping' and make special visits to retail outlets.

skimming the market   A pricing strategy that sets price at a high level to appeal to those customers for whom the product is highly desirable.

speciality products   Similar to *shopping goods*; products for which customers make shopping expeditions. If they are industrial products, they are called *technical specialities*.

staples   A class of consumer products that are frequently bought and are regarded as essential.

stock-turn   A statistical measurement indicating the number of times *average stock* is sold during a year.

stuffers   Small advertising leaflets and *folders* that are enclosed with letters, invoices, statements and other communications sent to customers and potential customers.

suspects   Those who it is thought may become buyers of a product or service.

target market   A part of the total market regarded as likely to buy, or to be capable of buying, a product.

threshold of perception   People's natural barrier between unawareness and awareness, which has to be bridged by advertisers who wish to stimulate interest in their product or service.

undifferentiated marketing   A strategy that ignores any possible market segmentation and has one marketing mix regarded as appropriate to the total market.

value-analysis   An estimate of the worth of a product based on costing and evaluating it.

value-pricing   Setting the price of a product according to what it is estimated that customers will pay for it.